NORTH WEST LONDON

Edited by Donna Samworth

First published in Great Britain in 2003 by
YOUNG WRITERS
Remus House,
Coltsfoot Drive,
Peterborough, PE2 9JX
Telephone (01733) 890066

SB ISBN 1 84460 219 2

FOREWORD

Young Writers was established in 1991 as a foundation for promoting the reading and writing of poetry amongst children and young adults. Today it continues this quest and proceeds to nurture and guide the writing talents of today's youth.

From this year's competition Young Writers is proud to present a showcase of the best poetic talent from across the UK. Each hand-picked poem has been carefully chosen from over 66,000 'Hullabaloo!' entries to be published in this, our eleventh primary school series.

This year in particular we have been wholeheartedly impressed with the quality of entries received. The thought, effort, imagination and hard work put into each poem impressed us all and once again the task of editing was a difficult but enjoyable experience.

We hope you are as pleased as we are with the final selection and that you and your family will continue to be entertained with *Hullabaloo! North West London* for many years to come.

CONTENTS

Sadia Latif	78
Dareon Hanlon	78
Valerie Amissah	79
Nathan Omar Gray	80
Haider Bashir	80
Llimahl Okocha	81
Candice Falconer	81
Kanyin Fagade	82
Domonique Smith	82
Matthew Kendall	83
Chezney Cassell	83
Lamar Charlemagne	84
Patrice King	84
Antonia Jones	85
Rochelle Hylton	86
Terrisa Bennett	86
Daisy Luyiga	87
Chanté Burrows	87
Kane Pfeiffer	88
Shaina Quaye-Iskander	88
Oyinka Bolatiwa	89
Nicole Mumuni	89
Mickaela Moore	90
Sarai Stern	90
Nicole Murray	91
Sherica Matthews	91
Jhonelle Williams	92
Jonathan Williams	93

Lyndhurst House School

Felix Cadieu	93
Adam Gigi	94
Guy Hayakawa	94
Sam Berrick	94
Hugo Woodhead	95
Lucien Cadieu	95
Tarik Basri	96
Gregory Dagul	96
Mark Mindel	97

The Poems

HELL'S MUSIC

Hell's music rings in my ears
The cries of men as they are shot
Their bodies fall in pools of blood
They lie there, floating.

Hell's music echoes in my brain,
The sounds of guns pounding into flesh
Bombs exploding and men flying
Screaming, as they are blown apart.

Hell's music screaming in my face,
The sobs of men at night,
As they cry for their loved ones at home
And their friends they have lost in battle.

I wish Hell's music would stop
In my dreaded days of life,
As I go to sleep hearing it
I dream it and wake to it,
Still hearing that dreadful sound
Of Hell's music.

Annabelle Sacher (10)

THE DOG

A soft, calmly relaxed dog, sits by the fire,
Every time he takes a breath
I see his best desire.
He likes to fall asleep and dream of dinner that night,
He is an old dog, full of might.

Georgia Jazz Summers (9)
Abercorn School

CIVILISATION

The building starts, a new city gets a heart,
The man blows a horn, a civilisation is born.
They have a peace treaty, the city is hearty,
The people have shown, they are not alone.
The civilians have great strife,
The city has had a long life.
The city is huge, there is no refuge,
No help is needed, the haven has succeeded.
The city is at war, the people start to bore,
The war is over, the people are starting to buy a Rover.
The city's technology has grown, the king is overthrown.
It is 2056, the people can mix
The people are bad, they have started to go mad.
The fabulous feast is on, the peace has gone.

Michael Russell (11)
Abercorn School

MY FRIEND'S HORSE

My friend has a horse called Bunny,
Which cost a lot of money.
And she can do a cross-country course
In less than ten minutes.

In the past
She's been really fast,
But now she's even faster!
It must be great to have a horse like that,
But I'm so happy, I have my cat.

Phoebe Norton (9)
Abercorn School

RUNNING

Running is the best
Better than all the rest,
Your stitch won't let you down
When you're running over a ditch.

I love to run
It is my passion,
Every day I dream
Of becoming the greatest champion.

You can't beat the feeling,
It really is impossible,
The running will make you strong
For any cross-country run.

Ori Tamir (9)
Abercorn School

THE HOMELESS DOG

He creeps into the kitchen to steal some tasty delicious,
glorious dog food,
Suddenly the dog's owner jumps and snatches the food from him.

Instead of slapping him like he usually does
His owner throws him out onto the disgusting,
wet, polluted street.

The dog hangs his head in shame,
He is not only hungry but also homeless.

Gordon Stewart (9)
Abercorn School

SCHOOL

A school has
Teachers,
Head teacher
Classrooms,
Blackboard . . .
But no students . . .

Ksenia Levina (9)
Abercorn School

CATS

Cats
Smelling food
Playing with a wool ball
Sleeping on the floor
Climbing trees
An active life
But *no* Whiskas!

Berlinda Middleton (9)
Abercorn School

TRUCK

Truck
Noisy
Fast moving
Carries a lot
Slow moving
Quiet
Still.

Danna Elmasry (8)
Abercorn School

IN A DEEP DARK CASTLE

In a deep, dark castle
You can see a shadow
If you follow that shadow
You will discover a deep, dark room.
If you follow a sign, it will lead you to a box.
In that box, your family will be waiting for you.

Milos Janjuševic (8)
Abercorn School

NEIGHBOURS FROM HELL

If you know neighbours from Hell
and my neighbours as well,
you'll probably agree
this is you and me
that they are neighbours from Hell!

George Richardson (10)
Abercorn School

IT WAS THE BEST MEAL I EVER HAD

It was the best meal I ever had,
My mouth watered.
We went to the fish and chip shop,
They served the most mouth-bursting sausages ever!
When I went home, I ate the chips and the cod
And in the smallest bites, the sausage.

Angus Smith (8)
Abercorn School

GOODBYE

The time has come to say goodbye
To my loving, elder sister

I began to think of the days with my sister
Playing games and catching each other

Although we would argue and fight and shout at each other
I still feel sorry for my loving, elder sister

She was caring
She was smart
She always made me laugh
I know I will never forget her
Until the world lasts

I started to cry
I started to sigh
And I started to think I've done nothing for her
I will write a letter
I will give her a picture
So she can remember us forever

The time has come to say goodbye
To my loving, elder sister

I gave her a big hug
With tears rolling down my cheek
And whispered, 'Goodbye!'

Rachel Yoo (11)
Abercorn School

WHY?

Why is the sun the colour of cheese?
Why is it rude if you don't say please?
Why are holidays shorter than terms?
Why are brothers made up of germs?

Why does God allow maths to exist?
Why is ice cream so hard to resist?
Why do grown-ups live mainly off tea?
Dad, *Dad* - are you listening to me?

Julia Taylor (9)
Abercorn School

THE OLD DOG

Look at the dog who is lying in the street
Too tired to chase the cat from Barnabus Road.

He doesn't chase the postman every Monday morning,
He doesn't pick the bones put out on Thursday mornings.

The old dog
Too tired to walk, too tired to bark -
So sad, so thin, with nothing to eat.

Sanya R Ahmed (9)
Abercorn School

THE LONG WALK

It was a long walk
I was very thirsty,
There was no water fountain around,
All there was, was burned grass.
The sun was playing tricks on my eyes
My feet were burning.
I was sweating like a pig
It felt like the water in my stomach was boiling
I could not wait to get home.

Justin Shapiro (9)
Abercorn School

SEASONS

Spring is the time for growth
Sun starts to come out
With a bit of a shout
And the breeze brings out the smell of fresh air.

Summer is the time for a holiday,
Spain, Italy, Egypt so hot - it's worth it to pay.
We've finished school
Now it's time to play in the swimming pool.

Autumn is the time of falling leaves,
The leaves turn brown, dropping in heaves.
The days get shorter and everything stops growing
It's dark, even when four o'clock is showing.

Winter is the time for the freeze and snow,
But Christmas is coming up, you know!
People rush to get their presents
To make each other happy and the season pleasant.

Nima Zad (11)
Abercorn School

THE OCEAN

The ocean is the calmest place, to brace the sounds of the ocean waves,
Dolphins flipping everywhere, you could just stand and stare,
The whole night, the whole day, it is just a beautiful place.
Kids and babies playing in the sand, making castles, oh how grand!
And you just sit there, relaxing, watching, as the sun sets
                                    in a ball of orange.

Talar Bilemjian (10)
Abercorn School

My Family

If my grandpa was a tree,
He would be a big willow tree,
With long branches
And his leaves would droop in the water.

If my grandma was an object,
She would be a ship,
Called Kingfisher,
And she would glide across the sea.

If my auntie was an animal,
She would be a dormouse
With a long pink tail
And she would scuttle around looking for food.

If my uncle was a bird
He would be a kingfisher
With metallic green feathers, shining in the sun
And he would dive down into the water.

If my dad was an animal,
He would be a monkey
With a great big hairy chest
And he would make funny monkey noises.

If my mum was a fruit,
She would be a cherry.
With a big red stalk, hanging out from the top
And she would sit on top of vanilla milkshakes all day.

If I was an animal,
I would be a rabbit
With a fluffy white tail and great big long ears,
And I would go hoppety-skippety down the path.

Sarika Ambasna (10)
Abercorn School

EXAMS AT ELEVEN O'CLOCK

Tick-tock, tick-tock,
Exams at eleven o'clock.
Tick-tock, tick-tock,
Exams at eleven o'clock!
I feel nervous,
I feel itchy
I feel frightened
I feel twitchy!

Tick-tock, tick-tock,
Exams at eleven o'clock.
Tick-tock, tick-tock,
Exams at eleven o'clock!
I feel sick
And I feel weak,
Got some homework,
Take a peek!

Tick-tock, tick-tock,
Exams at eleven o'clock.
Tick-tock, tick-tock,
Exams at eleven o'clock!

Madeleine Bennett (9)
Abercorn School

BOOKS

Front covers
Great illustrations
Huge hits
No pages!

Alanna Dent (8)
Abercorn School

MY MAGIC BOX
(Based on 'Magic Box' by Kit Wright)

My magic box
Is made with pearls
And can fit in my pocket.

My magic box
Can hold anything
Because it is magic.

My magic box
Has inside it -
Memories, treasures and things.

My magic box
Has an inside padded with velvet
And lots of secret compartments.

My magic box
Has a lock made out of gold
And a silver key.
My magic box.

Matthew Oswald (10)
Abercorn School

CLASSROOM

Hard desks
Paper books
Pretty pencils
Grand pens
A whiteboard as white as a cloud
But . . .
No teachers and no students!

Alice Haguenauer (9)
Abercorn School

MY CRAVING

A delicious bar
Chocolate mousse
A twist of whisky
Milky and mouth-watering
A massive craving.

But no chocolate!

Alexia Frangakis (8)
Abercorn School

SCHOOL

Students running around,
Break time for children.
Always in their uniforms
Classes all around . . .
No grown-ups!

Natalia Kyõko Toyama Green (8)
Abercorn School

THE TUBE

Tube
Fast-train
Un-der-ground
Lots-of-peo-ple
White-and-blue
Dri-ver
Fast!

Harley Fleming (9)
Abercorn School

THE STORM

The thunder clashed, the lightning flashed
and the rain fell on my head
I was getting wet, I started to fret
so I decided to go to bed

I woke up the next morning
the storm had stopped, however
There was lots of snow and a great big show
of the biggest snowman ever

You can imagine my delight
not a cloud in sight
But it started to pour (what a bore!)
so I'm going home early tonight.

Annie Wogel (9)
Abercorn School

THE SNOWMAN

The snowman I made was cold and big,
With coal for his eyes and arms made of twigs.
He was frosty and white from top to bottom,
So fluffy he looked, like three balls of cotton.
He had a long carrot for his nose
And was fat and round from his head to his toes.
His scarf was tucked under his chin,
In a snowman competition I think he would win.
Tomorrow will be a warm, sunny day,
Too bad my snowman will melt away.

Elisa Naini (10)
Abercorn School

FRIENDS OR FOES

Friends are the people whom you can trust,
Foes are the people who treat you like dust.
Friends are the people who are always there for you,
Foes are the people who always say, 'Boo!'
Friends are the people who never laugh at you,
Foes are the people who think you are a blob of goo.
Friends are the people who always never lie,
Foes are people whom you want to say goodbye to.
Friends are something you should treasure,
Foes are something that give you no pleasure.
So choose the right friends and you will find,
That these friends are always the right kind.

Xin Nee Ho (10)
Abercorn School

HORSES

Horses are gallant, beautiful and smooth,
I like the way that they move.
Trotting along the dusty golden sand,
Moving towards a brand new land.
Black, white and brown, they all differ in colour
But in many ways, similar to each other.
They are animals of the wild,
They are free
Just like you would dream to be.

Malak Kader (10)
Abercorn School

ALL YOU NEED IS . . .

I was feeling lonely that day,
My best friend had gone away.
The person I talked to, gossiped with and laughed.
And then came an apparition, a wonderful thing,
A girl who had nobody, who seemed alone.
She smiled and I smiled back, our eyes met
I can tell you without a bet, we hit it off from there,
And have been friends for over a year.

I was happy from then on
There was no need to be cheered up by tea cakes or bonbons.
I had a friend, a friend, a wonderful thing
Oh I could sing, sing, sing and sing!

I now never feel lonely
I never feel down,
I never have reason to moan or frown.
This is all because I have a friend,
Someone to help me round the bend.
Someone to guide me, lead and support,
That's all I need, nothing else, nothing more.
But remember friends can't be bought!

There's no way round it, all you can do
Is sit tight and wait your turn.
Friendship doesn't come if you bribe or you plead,
But wait your turn and you will succeed.
A friend is all anybody needs!

Georgia Sheeran (10)
Abercorn School

KIDS

Kids, kids like to jump and play,
They do this more than every day.
They scrape their knees and poke their eyes,
They need supplies just to survive,
What can we do?
They ask for some sweets and do gigantic leaps
Just so they look so cool,
But really they look like a fool.
I wonder if when I was a kid I acted
Just the same,
Older kids must have thought I was really lame,
I wish I was never born!

Morenike Graham-Douglas (9)
Abercorn School

MY WINGED DRAGON

My winged dragon can fly so high
That he can even touch the sky

My winged dragon loves to learn
And sometimes he pretends to be Albert Einstein

My winged dragon loves to play sport
And his favourite sport is basketball

I love my dragon, so please don't take
His lovely smile away from me.

David Coates (11)
Abercorn School

A Cold Dark Room

We stepped into the cold, dark room,
The floor started to creak.
There were cobwebs everywhere and dust flew around the room.
Footsteps could be heard from downstairs,
Our hearts turned into stone.

There was a thunderstorm outside the window,
Rats were crawling everywhere.
The cold, dark room was overgrown with ivy,
The chairs looked like ghosts with white cloths
It was so cold -
And we couldn't wait to get out.

Trent Forrister (9)
Abercorn School

Solo Act

I am an acrobat, daring and bold,
I razzle, I dazzle in a suit made of gold.
The clowns are way down there, pulling my strings,
As I glide through the air, as if I had wings.
The crowd is so silent, their eyes filled with hope,
While I dance and I prance on this high trapeze rope.
The performers are funny - some skinny, some fat.
But none please the crowd as I -
The sparkling,
Tumbling
Acrobat.

Jack Begert (9)
Abercorn School

BOYS

Boys are wacky, sometimes cool,
Sometimes funny, but not at school.
Boys are good at techno games,
But not at all at crossword games,
Boys are fast but sometimes slow,
But sometimes none of any of those.
So this is what I think of boys,
But I still think girls are *better* then *cool!*

Courtney Lovejoy (10)
Abercorn School

I WISH . . .

I wish Christmas would come every week,
I wish my mum would always play a game.
I wish I didn't always eat meat
I wish everyone looked the same.

I wish I had a racing car,
I wish my puppy could breathe fire.
I wish I was a bright star,
I wish I was a yellow spider.

I wish I could be Miss Pulley
I wish my brother would shrink.
I wish my cousin wasn't a bully
I wish my brain didn't have to think.

But the most important wish of all
Is that I want to be very tall!

Edgar Da Silva (9)
Deansbrook Junior School

I WISH

I wish my hair was lively and straight
I wish I didn't wear braces,
I wish I was known as Mairead the Great
I wish I knew how to do shoe laces.

I wish I was a super girl
Who had the powers of nature,
I wish I was the girl who had a little curl,
Right in the middle of her forehead,
So I could be a pretty picture.

I wish we could bring back the dead
So I could have my dog, Boxty,
I wish right now I could pat him on the head
I wish I wasn't such a softie!

Mairead McNulty (9)
Deansbrook Junior School

WISH, WISH, WISH

I wish, I wish I had a big fish,
I wish, I wish I wasn't such a dish.
I wish that my writing could be neat
I wish and I wish I didn't have such smelly feet!

I wish my mum wouldn't nag and nag and nag!
I wish that I was tall
I wish that my dad wouldn't have a fag
I wish my dad didn't smoke
I wish that I was better at basketball
I wish that I was you!

Aaron Foster
Deansbrook Junior School

MY WISH POEM

I wish I were a fat pig
I wish I could eat goo
I wish I could dig
I wish I were called Boo.

I wish I were a cup
I wish I could walk
I wish I had a lamp
I wish I could talk.

I wish I were a cop
I wish I had a car
I wish I were at the top
I wish I could go far.

I wish I were bread,
I wish I were thin
I wish I could spread
I wish I had a fin.

I wish I were a cake
I wish I had a fox
I wish I could bake
I wish I had rocks.

Kayachris Weekes (9)
Deansbrook Junior School

WISH, WISH, WISH

I wish I could step into the TV once in a while,
I wish I could fly very high.
I wish my brother's name was Kyle,
I wish I could make apple pie.

I wish I could creep like a mouse
I wish Christmas was every day,
I wish I had a flying house
I wish I could jumbo jet to the USA.

Laura Spenceley (8)
Deansbrook Junior School

THE BOY WHO WISHES

I wish I were a superstar
I wish I could drive a van
I wish I could go to a bar
I wish I could flip food in a pan

I wish I could flow like a river
I wish I were in a tree
I wish I could slither like a snake
I wish dogs wouldn't pee on me

I wish I had loads of money
I wish I could be a horse
I wish I could buy some honey
I wish I wouldn't run around the course.

I wish my name were Chester
I wish I were a plant
I wish I were a wrestler
I wish my mum would stopping saying 'I shan't.'

I wish I spoke every language
I wish I didn't have a book
I wish I didn't eat that sandwich
I wish I could put my book in the cook.

Nick Brown (8)
Deansbrook Junior School

WISH, WISH, WISH

I wish I could talk to chimps, far away,
I wish I could go into space, without dying.
I wish I had a very good spectacular day
I wish everyone would stop lying.

I wish I was faster than a Ford Escort
I wish I was a hobbit like Frodo,
I wish I could escape to the airport,
I wish there was no such word as *no!*

Saqib Din (9)
Deansbrook Junior School

WISH, WISH, WISH

I wish I had a bike which was lucky
I wish my birthday was every day,
I wish I could swing like a monkey
I wish I could go to the USA.

I wish I could fly high in the sky
I wish I had a magic hat,
I wish my sister didn't lie
I wish I was a bat.

Leanne Lynch (9)
Deansbrook Junior School

WISH, WISH, WISH

I wish Christmas came every day
I wish I had a golden stretch limo
I wish I could sprout my wings and fly away
I wish I could do the limbo

I wish my name was Ben
I wish my sister would shrink
I wish I was a big bad hen
I wish I had a magic drink.

Becki Ellingham
Deansbrook Junior School

WISH, WISH, WISH

I wish I was Harry Potter
I wish I had a cat or dog
I wish I had a pound of butter
I wish I was stuck in a bog

I wish it was character day
I wish I had a brother
I wish it was Christmas every day
I wish I had a sister
I wish I was you!

Chris Coyle (8)
Deansbrook Junior School

WISH, WISH

I wish I could never die and
Spread golden wings and fly high in the sky.
I wish my mother would give birth and
I would have a baby brother.

I wish I had a house of gold
I wish I had a lizard strong and bold.
I wish I was the strongest man in the world.

Jordan Heron (9)
Deansbrook Junior School

I Wish

I wish I had a new house
I wish my teeth were straight,
I wish I had a pet mouse
I wish I had a best mate.

I wish I had a good book
I wish I had a big room,
I wish I had a new look
I wish I heard a boom.

I wish I had a sister called Angelica
I wish I could say, 'Boo!'
I wish I lived in America
I wish I heard a cow go 'Moo!'

I wish I had small ears
I wish I was at a zoo,
I wish I could say, 'Cheers!'
I wish I was you!

Robbie Hale (8)
Deansbrook Junior School

I Wish

I wish I had a boyfriend
I wish I was very clever,
I wish I could mend
I wish there was no such word as never.

I wish I was in Page
I wish I had a big house.
I wish my friends didn't fly into a rage
I wish I had a pet mouse.

I wish I didn't have a big spam
I wish I was a millionaire,
I wish I went to a field with a baby lamb
I wish there was a fair.

I wish I could be eighteen forever
I wish there was more homework
I wish I'd found a multicoloured fiver
I wish I was you!

Demi Smart (9)
Deansbrook Junior School

RIDICULOUS POEM

I wish I were a secret spy
I wish I ate spaghetti pie
I wish I had some gadgets
I wish I had more budgets

I wish I built aircraft
I wish I wasn't daft
I wish I had a submarine
I wish I joined the super marines

I wish war would come to an end
I wish I didn't live round the bend
I wish I were living in Lancaster
I wish my whistle would go 'Baster, baster!'

I wish I were taller
I wish I got bolder
I wish I built a pyramid
I wish my hands were lids.

Christopher Brown (8)
Deansbrook Junior School

WISH, WISH, WISH

I wish I owned a fast McLaren
I wish I travelled far
I wish I knew what to do
With the suspension of the car.

I wish I swam as quickly as I can.
I wish I never drowned.
I wish I was as good as Nick
So I could never feel sick
When I'm crowned.

I wish I were a football player
Who always played up front
I wish I always knew what to do
When I kick the ball from the start.

I wish I were a good goalie
Who always saved the shots
I wish I never let the ball in
So the other team wouldn't win.

Mahmoud Ata (9)
Deansbrook Junior School

WISH, WISH, WISH

I wish I were a classic football star.
I wish I played for the best team, Madrid.
I wish I were a good goal scorer,
I wish I were a kid.

I wish I had skill and balance.
I wish I could meet the Mayor.
I wish I had very good talents,
I wish I were a skilled football player.

I wish I had a black Ferrari.
I wish I had a CD player.
I wish I went on a safari,
I wish I had a friend called Frayer.

I wish I had a bowl of honey.
I wish I had a bag of gold.
I wish I had a big bag of money,
I wish I were a little bold.

Jack Mardell (9)
Deansbrook Junior School

A GIRL THING

I wish I were popular.
I wish I had straight hair.
I wish I could be Britney Spears.
I wish I were a star.

I wish I were a teacher.
I wish I had a laptop.
I wish I had a whiteboard.
I wish I were an author.

I wish I were Queen.
I wish I were a princess.
I wish I ruled all of England.
I wish I had a throne.

I wish my dad were Homer.
I wish my mum were Marge.
I wish my brother were Bart.
I wish I were Lisa.
I wish my sister were Maggie.

Mahnoor Khan
Deansbrook Junior School

WISH, WISH, WISH

I wish for a big house
I wish for a brother
I wish I was as quiet as a mouse
I wish I was in bed, under the covers.

I wish I could like school,
I wish my handwriting was neat.
I wish for a magical pencil
I wish I could give the music some beat.

I wish I was a millionaire
I wish I was a scientist,
I wish I didn't stare.
I wish I was you.

Matthew Cobley (9)
Deansbrook Junior School

I WISH

I wish I was as quiet as a mouse
I wish I had a big house.
I wish I had my toys all to myself
I wish I had an uncle.
I wish I had a big dog,
I wish I had a small teacher.
I wish I had my name changed
My name was Iain
I wish I looked like Mrs Healy.

Dilesh Tanna (9)
Deansbrook Junior School

WISH, WISH, WISH

I wish I didn't wear glasses,
I wish I could do magic.
I wish my shoes didn't have laces
I wish my mum was not scared of maggots.

I wish I didn't need to work,
I wish my guinea pig was still alive.
I wish I didn't burp
I wish I had stayed fire.

I wish my mum was called Kate,
I wish I didn't go to school.
I wish I had lots of mates
I wish I was you.

Adam Taie (9)
Deansbrook Junior School

WISH, WISH, WISH

I wish I could talk to animals.
I wish I was Ron Weasley.
I wish I could go to a carnival.
I wish I could do homework easily.

I wish I had a pet owl.
I wish I had a chocolate land.
I wish I had a pal.
I wish I had six hands.

Beau Mehmet
Deansbrook Junior School

WISH, WISH, WISH

I wish my sister was not annoying
I wish we could do anything in class,
I wish my house got lots of house points
I wish I could run really fast.

I wish I had lots of sweets
I could eat them on the way back from school
I wish I could wear funky boots
I would look really cool.

I wish I wore glasses
I wish we wore a tie for school
I wish I had a pencil case like Abigail and Camilla
I am not a fool!

India Heath (8)
Deansbrook Junior School

WISH, WISH, WISH

I wish I could run as fast as a car
And not be last.
I wish I could fly in the sky.
I wish I could be good at football.
I wish for a magic car.
I wish my cat could learn to say fat.
I wish I had a game that was the same.
I wish I had a dog that could learn to say log.
I wish we could have Christmas every week.
I wish I was Santa.

Chelsea Wells (9)
Deansbrook Junior School

MY WISH

I wish I were a super star.
I wish I came from Manchester.
I wish I were a fat king.
I wish I could have a gold ring.

I wish I could go to a magic shop.
I wish I had a goldfish.
I wish I could have a lollipop.
I wish I had a supper dish.

I wish I had a best mate.
I wish I had a crate.
I wish I could date.
I wish I could create.

Conor Staples
Deansbrook Junior School

WISH, WISH, WISH

I wish I could fly high in the sky,
I wish I met a cheetah named Peter,
I wish I had a fly that could make apple pie,
I wish I could meet a caterpiller named Anita.

I wish I was on the moon, eating with a spoon,
I wish I was a bird that could make lemon curd,
I wish I was a cartoon on the telly at noon.

Joseph Lalor (9)
Deansbrook Junior School

FIRE

I stand in a fire,
Blazing,
Glazing.
I stand in the smoke,
Ashy,
Trashy.
I stand,
I cry.
I see,
I see,
High in the sky,
Blazing,
Glazing,
Up and up it goes,
Down and down the house goes.
Blazing,
Glazing,
I hear the engines,
Whining,
Chinning,
I hear a baby cry,
'Waa, waa.'
A man screaming
'Save me,
Save me!'
Women screaming,
Streets ablazing,
Everyone in the street,
Out saving any little feet,
Blazing,
Glazing,
Saving everyone,
Hoses full blow,

Smoke a-rising,
Fire settling,
Everyone saved but . . .
The house!

Emily Ford (11)
Devonshire House Preparatory School

MY POEM TO BE SPOKEN SILENTLY

It was so silent that I heard . . .
The little mice scuttle along swiftly,
Across the garden path . . .

It was so quiet that I heard . . .
A bite of a crisp crackle,
In the dining room . . .

It was so calm and still,
I could see the devilish look on the raindrops
On the window sill . . .

It was so quiet that I heard . . .
A little shooting star zoom past,
It soon disappeared . . .

It was so peaceful that I felt . . .
The clock tick,
It was almost like it was speaking . . .

Thump! Thump!
Went the ants,
I really was confused . . .

Ashoke Sen (10)
Devonshire House Preparatory School

SWEETS!

Sweets are delicious
Unfortunately not nutritious!
Strawberry, chocolate, raspberry and cream.
Every sweet is surely supreme
Sweet and sour
You have to devour
The delicious, heavenly sweets.
They're something everyone eats.
Tall
Thin
Small
Fat
Chewy
Crunchy
Sweet
Sour . . .
'Mol, what are you doing in the fridge?'

Mollie Campsie (10)
Devonshire House Preparatory School

SHARK

Jaw-snapper
Fish-catcher
Dolphin-fighter
Sea-glider
Whale-fearer
Tail-shearer
Never-beaten
Ahhh! I've been eaten!

Amber Willis (10)
Devonshire House Preparatory School

In Mid Winter

(Inspired by 'In Just Spring' by E E Cummings)

In mid

Winter when the world is a muddy big ball

Bouncing up and *bang!*

And rain myriads of water pelting down and big buckets
of it too.

When the world from afar is a wet blue ball

In mid

Winter when the brown ball is bouncing up and *bang* and
the people come running wearing their waterproof skin and
plastic feet, buckets in hand hoping to catch the myriads of
water pelting down

In mid-winter when the world is a muddy big ball

Bouncing up and b . . .

Jess Linehan (10)
Devonshire House Preparatory School

The Snowball Fight

S oft squelchy snow
N aughty children
O dd-shaped snowballs
W et weird wonders
B ig balls roll
A ll over lies snow
L oud screams
L aughing mouths.

Ella Perry (9)
Devonshire House Preparatory School

MY POEM TO BE SPOKEN SILENTLY

It was so silent that I heard . . .
Foxes running about a mile away
And the trees playing with the grass,

It was so silent that I heard . . .
The cheese freeze
And heard dancing to the music,

It was so silent that I heard . . .
The tap sneezing with water,
And the rake scratching the table,

It was so silent that I heard . . .
The hammer bullying the screws
And the water crying,

It so was silent that I heard . . .
The trees dancing because of the wind
And the wind whistling.

Ben Lurie (10)
Devonshire House Preparatory School

MINI BEASTS ATTACK

Mini beasts roam the planet,
All looking for me.
There are spiders, ants, mosquitoes,
Even the bumblebee.

Spiders are like toilet brushes,
With legs like hairy pins.
Ants like soldiers marching,
All searching for my limbs.

Mosquitoes fly like vampires,
Their bite could pierce a stone.
Bees buzzing in their choirs,
All heading for my home.

Mini beasts are like tiny magnets,
All trying to drink my blood.
But I am out to get them,
I crush them with a *thud!*

Alice Alexander (10)
Devonshire House Preparatory School

CHILDREN

Children are like pages
Some run as fast as pages flicking,
Some walk as slow as one page turning.

Children are like animals
Some are as tall as giraffes,
Some are as short as dogs.

Children are like gold
Some are as sparkly as the sun,
Some are as hard as brick.

Children are like planets
Some are as hot as Mercury,
Some are as cold as Pluto.

Children are like stories
They all have different endings,
So do children's lives.

Melisa Erginbilgic (9)
Devonshire House Preparatory School

HORSES

H   orses, horses, as beautiful as can be
   riding in the sunshine and splashing in the sea.

O   bedient and graceful on the warm straw they lie
   the spirit of a horse will never ever die.

Riding through the quiet woods can be so much fun
   cantering and galloping through the four seasons' sun.

S   hining ever so brightly, a horse's soft warm coat
   jumping over puddles, rocks and maybe even a moat.

E   ver so elegantly walking proudly towards the shine
   feeling enormously happy and so very fine.

S   leeping ever so softly and quietly making not a sound
   waiting for the morning sun to rise and finally be found.

Zoe Kotsis (11)
Devonshire House Preparatory School

HUNGRY HENRY

It was the day of the big feast
When I met that irritating beast.
He ate the fruit, he ate the lot
And gurgled down some water out of a pot.
But then he fixed his eyes on me
And I knew that he could see
Me being a tasteful meal
So I started to scream and squeal
But then I caught a very big ferry
To get away from Hungry Henry.

Jack Brighouse (9)
Devonshire House Preparatory School

MOM'S HANDBAG

A melted lipstick
A broken watch
A boxing bag
A fishing net
And that's not all!
A bowling ball
A window sill
A blackboard
Sticky sweets
A bunch of flowers
A door handle . . .
'What Mom?'
'No, I can't carry your handbag.'
(I'm not a body builder!)

Irene Moraitis (11)
Devonshire House Preparatory School

WINTER

Snowflakes fall all around,
Soft and white on the ground,
Children laugh, run and play,
Faster, faster! On their sleighs!
Icicles hang from the trees,
Sharp and pointy as they freeze,
Rushing home for tea,
By the fire, watching TV,
Nice and warm in bed at night,
I hear my mama whisper . . . 'Sleep tight!'

Alice Dallin-Walker (11)
Devonshire House Preparatory School

SNOW

All was quiet, all was bright,
Then it started to snow.
What a sight!
Floating in the air the snow would go.

Down, down, down, went the snowflakes,
People slipping over,
Children building snowmen in their breaks,
People heading for cover.

Snowballs flying all over the playground,
Mountains of snow all around,
Teachers inside, safe and sound,
Snow falling down.

Sean Quah (9)
Devonshire House Preparatory School

THE MAGICIAN

Moustache twirler
Wand whirler

Rabbit snatcher
Smile catcher

Flag producing
Mirth inducing

Truth distorting
Gaily cavorting

Dazzling with delusion.

Rosa Bennathan (11)
Devonshire House Preparatory School

SNOW

The little children running around,
With the flying snow,
The really icy ground
Their little faces glow.

While little children scream and shout,
The tiny kids go flying about,
The teachers drink a secret stout,
While the playground turns into a boxing bout!

As big snowballs smash into their faces,
Their tears start to leak,
The snowballs being thrown at such a pace,
The winter weather is at its peak.

Elliot Leen (9)
Devonshire House Preparatory School

SNOW

Snow is like a blanket
It is as white as this paper
It is as cold as an ice box

Frost is like the icing on a cake
It is spread as ketchup on chips
It is as pretty as my mum

Icicles are like upside down candles
They are as shiny as silver
They are as glimmering as gold
They are as dazzling as diamonds.

Oliver John (10)
Devonshire House Preparatory School

FLOWERS

Flowers are like paintings.
They are as colourful as a
Rainbow.
They are as picturesque as
Trees.

Flowers are like perfume.
They are as fragrant as
Spring fresh air.

Some flowers are like
Statues.
They are as still as
Stone.
Dandelions are as fugitive
As the wind.

Flowers are lovely!

Arman Ghassemieh (9)
Devonshire House Preparatory School

THE OAK TREE

At the back of my garden
A big tree stands,
With lots of branches
Shaped like hands,
Different coloured leaves, green and brown,
In autumn they fall to the ground,
It is an oak tree with big brown bark,
From my window it looks scary in the dark.

Tianna Georcelin (10)
Leopold Primary School

GOING UP THE STAIRS

Going up the stairs in the dark, boo!
You get scared but what can you do?
Well, take someone with you,
Maybe them too!

Going up the stairs,
Seeing something white, maybe a ghost!
Or a postman when he sends his post.
Curtains moving from the wind,
As you hear a tomato tin.

Going up the stairs
Getting scared!
With the monster in the beard.
Argh!

Going up the stairs!

Saba Ali (9)
Leopold Primary School

THE UNHEALTHY AFRICAN MAN

The unhealthy African man seemed tired and bored.
He gazed towards Heaven and worshipped the great Lord.
Rowing each day, his shoulder became broad.
He left his blue boat and discovered a golden sword.

The waves crashing against the rock was all he heard.
He saw another ship sailing on the sea.
Starving and thirsty, he recovered a coconut tree.
He started to cry, how thankful he could be.

Another island day passed by. What appeared? *A bird.*

Iqra Zulfiqar (10)
Leopold Primary School

HIDE-AND-SEEK

We went to play hide-and-seek
2, 4, 6, 8,
And I'm on
And my eyes are not shut
10, 12, 14, 16,
And I'm counting
And they all might cheat
Except for me
18, 20, 22, 24,
I sometimes think
Just for a minute
26, 28, 30, 32,
Everyone all gone
And I've not found anyone
It's an empty world
34, 36, 38, 40,
And just the sky
Ready or not, here I come!

Jordan Boateng (9)
Leopold Primary School

THE LONELY MAN

The lonely man was sitting there looking very bored.
He looked at the sky and prayed to the Lord.
His shoulder looked weak but broad.
He looked at the coconut tree and saw a sword.
He cut a coconut saying, 'What was that behind me I heard?'
He felt very sad and hungry
So he looked towards the sky and prayed to the Lord.

Roshni Patel (9)
Leopold Primary School

GUNS

Guns are bad.
Why do we use them?
They just create war.
They just make you go to prison.
Why are people so horrible and have guns?
Nobody should have guns.
No more guns!
This must stop *now!*
We will make signs saying 'No more guns'.
We do not like *guns!*
People with guns kill other people
Please stop, you are killing our world,
We do not like you for that.
You will have no friends.
Think of all the people who have died because of guns.
       Let's stop this now!

Myron Forbes (9)
Leopold Primary School

THE MAGIC RAINBOW

A rainbow came upon my way,
A magic rainbow with colours gay.
It never stops shining bright,
Or even that special light.
It lights the world with pretty colours
And you can never see its end.
But you'll always know its special message,
But never hear its voice.

Motunrayo Fashipe (9)
Leopold Primary School

GOD

God has many gifts given by His Son
To all the people who live in the world.
God is all around the world.
At night He gives people wishes.
God, God, God, I love you.

There is only one God.
There is only one king.
There is only one body.
That is why we sing
'God, God, God, I love you.'
That is why we sing.

Sheneka Rhoden
Leopold Primary School

WISE UP YOUTH

What has happened to the youth today?
All the shooting has to stop right away,
I hear the policeman's feet coming down the street,
I feel the heat, the pounding of my feet,
My youth on the corner, he needs to make a deal,
But he'd rather steal. I jump into my jeep, I hear a beep,
I turn the corner, the police pull me over,
They pull me out of the car, if I run, I won't get far,
They search my jeep, they jump on the seat,
They find a gun, what a shock!

Kisha Millar (9)
Leopold Primary School

THE SKY

Soft,
White clouds
Slightly moving about
Aeroplanes about
Helicopters about
Airlines fade away
There's the blue sky.
Sun comes out
Sometimes
The rain scatters about
When it snows
That's when it's cold!
But the sky never changes
It never dies
Oh, the luscious sky!

Yolanda Dennis (9)
Leopold Primary School

THE LONELY MAN

The strong, lonely man seemed tired and bored
Gazing towards the clouds he prayed to the Lord
With all that paddling, his strong shoulders were broad
He searched through his boat to recover a sword
The crashing waves were all that he heard
He stared, amazed, at the rough sea
As he rested his boat beside the tree
And decided to close his eyes to plea
A song in the air of a beautiful bird.

Sheetal Bhudia (10)
Leopold Primary School

THE RIVER

Water going by
people on their boats
waves going by
so gently near houses
near villages

The water gets high
higher when you go by
imagine waves
going up
to the sky
green waves
blue waves
high as you can imagine
yes, you can,
if you try.

Chrystal Cassell (9)
Leopold Primary School

THE LONELY MAN

The strong, lonely man looked tough and bored
He gazed strongly towards the Lord
With all that worry the lucky, strong shoulders were broad
He perched over his boat and discovered there was his sword
The man heard the roaring of the waves
The man heard the rippling sea.
Then he looked at the palm tree
He invoked again and pleaded
He gazed at the flying bird.

Rasvita Patel (10)
Leopold Primary School

LUMBLY

Lumbly and delight
Don't forget to sleep tight
Under my sleepyhead chin,
I hope you understand
I am not the person you are looking for.

The moon is,
The moon is under my chin,
The birds won't, they won't stop singing
And the storm, the storm won't stop blowing.

Lumbly and delight,
Don't forget to sleep tight,
Under my sleepyhead chin,
I hope you understand
I am not the person you are looking for.

The moon is,
The moon is under my chin,
The birds won't, they won't stop singing
And the storm, the storm won't stop blowing.

Ashleigh Christie (9)
Leopold Primary School

SORRY

Sorry is a way of showing pity,
Like when you accidentally kick your kitty,
You quickly say sorry,
But they don't understand,
So they just come and bite off your hand.

Daniel Murray (11)
Leopold Primary School

THE BEACH

By the sand
Ice cream dripping
Seashells glistening
Wavy water
Nice hot sun
In the fun
Swimming in the water
Swimming costumes
Yellow sand
Spades digging
Sandcastle making
On the beach

Devina Russell-Rhoden (9)
Leopold Primary School

THE BEACH

Splish, splash, all over my feet
Soaking wet
As I eat
Splish, splash, freezing cold
Ice cream dripping
On the golden shore
As I read there goes more
Splish, splash, burning hot
Rain coming
Cooling me down
Splish, splash, soaking wet.

Tamika Warner (10)
Leopold Primary School

THE RIVER

Shallow
Children eating
Lovely views
Glows in the dark
Always cold
Sometimes curly
Smashing, bashing
Can't stop flowing
Can't stop growing
Shining in the sun
People laughing
Having fun
Fishes swimming
Crackling and bubbling
The river!

Dami Owolana (10)
Leopold Primary School

THE BEACH

Golden sand
Big waves
Children playing
Lots of candy
People surfing
People swimming
Kids having fun
The sand is hot
The beach is fun.

Anthony Dingwall (9)
Leopold Primary School

War! War!

War, war, why the war? Can't we all just have peace and harmony?
War, war, why the war? I don't understand,
War, war, why the war? I often ask myself,
War, war, why the war? I don't know!

Every day on the news, war, war, war,
You never get anything different, just war, war, war, war,
Guns, knives, pistols make . . . *war, war, war!*
Why the war? Why the war, war, war, war?

Everything leads to war, war, war,
Racism leads to war, war, war,
War is a deadly thing that everybody should hate
War kills and I hate it!

Why did Hitler die? Because of war, war, war,
All President Bush wants is war, war, war,
All Tony Blair wants is war, war, war,
Even police, all they want is war, war, war,

This message is to . . . s*top war!*

Khalid Shillingford (10)
Leopold Primary School

Football Speaks

I'm something round,
not always on the ground.
I bounce and bounce
and move around.

I go high,
sometimes I fly.
I make people cry.
I make people try.

I'm hit.
I'm beat.
I don't care,
it's something I can bear.

'Cause when you're living life like me,
it's something you will see -
you will try and call out
that I'm a football.

Kene Agbasimelo (10)
Leopold Primary School

No More Wars!

No more wars, please, please!
People will die, children will cry,
Why? Because of the war!
People have no lives
Seeing guns and knives.
Children looking for their mums and dads.

People cry and say goodbye to loved ones,
Saying goodbye is hard for them,
So they cry, 'I cannot die.'
So we say, 'No more wars!'

God will help stop this,
We will help too,
So we'll not see people dying anymore,
Make it happy for them,
Make it happy for me,

So no more war!

Christine Antubam (10)
Leopold Primary School

MAKE LONDON SAFE

London, London,
The big city of London
If you want to be safe
You won't get shot in the face.

Shooting, stealing, smoking weed,
Won't get you far,
The police will get you
So you will end up behind bars.

Remember Londoners,
Never shoot, steal or smoke weed
London, London,
The big city of London.

Sharelle Williams (10)
Leopold Primary School

THE SKY

Blue clouds
blazing sun

Kids playing
having fun

Neighbours moaning
angry mums

The sky is fluffy
it's nice, beautiful
and blue.

The sky!

Kadeem Graham (9)
Leopold Primary School

THE RIVER

Soft
Very cold
Picnics
Water
More and more of it
Blue and green
Plants and people
Others too
So soft
The river
Very quiet
While passing by
Water, water
Very cool
So soft.
The river!

Triseena White (9)
Leopold Primary School

THE RIVER

Wavy
Cold and windy
Pictures of the shore
Swans and ducks
In the river
The river is
So nice and smooth
That's why I like
The river!

Kamilah Hardie (10)
Leopold Primary School

MY FOOTBALL CRIED LAST NIGHT

My football cried last night,
So I asked him, 'Are you all right?'
He said, 'No.'
I said, 'Oh no.'
I asked him,
'Is it because of Jim?'
'It is because,' he blazed,
'You're so hard, you got crazed.'
He said, 'Yes.'
I told him that
He will play
Football for a week.
He said, 'You're the best,
In the west
And better than the rest.'

Jamal Finni (10)
Leopold Primary School

THE RIVER

Calm and quiet
otters and swans
people laughing
blue and green glistening
everlasting
picnics on the sand
lying in the sun
as the ripples glow
oh, I love the river!

Paris McNeil (10)
Leopold Primary School

THE CLOWN

Shiny red nose
Extra large-sized feet
A small little rose
Pulls away when you meet
Big creamy pies
People laugh
Throw it in his eyes
Throw the hose, he's bathing
Big red and green hair
With big baggy trousers
Makes him a bear
Laughing loud, hours and hours.
        That's the clown!

Patricia Kibuuka-Musoke (9)
Leopold Primary School

WHAT I WONDER ABOUT

I wonder why the grass is the colour green
And why the wind is impossible to be seen?
Why do birds build some nests
And why do we need to rest?
Everyday I wonder about things,
Like clues, why is a clue called a clue?
I wonder why trees are made out of wood
And why my poem is not understood?
There are a lot of things to wonder about,
Like cats and hats and school being cool.
Then suddenly I sit still and just stop
Wondering!

Opeyemi Adenaike (11)
Leopold Primary School

IN THE CLASSROOM

In my classroom, happy classroom
children are proud and free,
some even work as if they are teachers.
The boys are keen to work and help
and the girls are clean and keen to learn.

We learn, learn, learn
and the teacher is lovingly stern,
we have computer time
and we write poems which rhyme.

We go outside and run,
and it is so much fun,
in and out of the classroom,
learning is always fun.

Emmanuel Adjerese (10)
Leopold Primary School

THE RECIPE OF WITCHES

Thrice the mice of the mixed rice,
More and more, it's nice, it's mice.
Tumble over, 'tis cauldron,
Make a big rumble to make it bubble,
Row, row, row the cauldron, thrice and thrice,
Make it bubble with rice mice, nice,
Double trouble, I'm in trouble,
Cut me loose and make thou swell,
Right, right, right, I'm breathing into fright.

Michelle-Ann Olivia Jobson (11)
Leopold Primary School

THE BEACH

Golden sand
On the beach,
Very nice and hot,
Right on the spot,
Glancing sun,
Having fun,
Making sandcastles
On a very warm day,
In the swimming pool,
Then out, cool,
Dig, dig, dig,
Golden sand.

Vaughan Anderson Moore (9)
Leopold Primary School

TEACHERS!

Teachers, teachers,
Never groan and moan,
They go home.
Here's a chant from the kids,
Very well teachers, go home!
Don't come back till you're grown.
Let's go party,
Let's get groovy,
Let's tease moody.
Oh teachers back to normal self,
We're in trouble, let's go home.
That's teacher for you, 'Yeah!'

Samantha McLeod (10)
Leopold Primary School

CHILDREN HAVE A RIGHT

All children have a right
to do something new in their lives.
They have a right to protest when things go wrong
and grow up to be husbands and wives.

Adults were children once
and they had rights to do stuff.
But now they won't let us be on our own,
even when things go rough.

I really like being a child,
but sometimes things are not fair
and it seems like parents
hardly ever, care.

But being a child is very hard,
even though school is not.
Sometimes people act as if you don't exist.
They act as if you are just a little dot
and I think:
all children have a right!

Pamela Ogboro (10)
Leopold Primary School

SORRY

S   is for sincerity.
O   is for overlooking your problems.
R   is for respecting other people's feelings.
R   is for rethinking your wrongs.
Y   is for yelling you're *sorry!*

Michaela Nadine Forbes (10)
Leopold Primary School

HARLESDEN, KEEP IT SAFE!

Every night I hear the sounds of horrible,
Terrifying sounds in Harlesden.

Screaming, banging, swearing,
Seems endless, the sounds no lesser.

Shouting, rowing, dreadful laughing,
It sounds like World War III is coming on.

Wheezing, crying, squealing,
It sounds like a drug addict.

Growling, quarrelling, despicable behaviour,
It sounds like an alcoholic.

Every day when I go out,
I hear people bad naming Harlesden.
All children see in Harlesden is malicious people fighting
And policemen.

If you want people to love you
And Harlesden,
Keep it safe!

Nicolle Zoë Franklin (11)
Leopold Primary School

PEACE

P   olite is very good.
E   veryone is not perfect.
A   chieving is clever.
C   areful is being safe.
E   asy-peasy is an expression.

Taiye Fashipe (8)
Leopold Primary School

THE BEACH

The beach is cool
The beach is refreshing
Balls bouncing
Golden sand
Spades are digging
Buckets upside down
Ice cream dripping
White shells sparkle
Candyfloss fizzing
Swimming in the sea
Bathing on the sand
Golden sand
The beach.

Joy Azu (9)
Leopold Primary School

THE BEACH

Hot,
So hot,
Ice cream melting,
Waves so high,
Laughing, chattering,
While people pass by,
Spades are digging,
Buckets are full,
People splash water,
Up and down,
Ball bounces,
On the golden shore
Of the beach.

Latoya Phillips (10)
Leopold Primary School

WAITING FOR MY SISTER

I'm standing in the playground,
I am waiting alone,
My sister isn't coming
And I'm thinking of my home.

I am standing in the playground,
I'm waiting by the gate.
The teachers are all going
And it's getting very late.

The playground is nearly empty,
There's no one left to play.
I am getting rather frightened
And I don't know what to say.

My name is Abigail Gyesi,
My sister's name is Zoe Kpodo,
Cos I am only 17.

Abigail Gyesi (8)
Leopold Primary School

CHRISTMAS POETRY

C   hristmas has come
H   ome is full of cheer
R   euben is very excited
I   s he waiting for Father Christmas to appear?
S   now, snow, snow, the snow is falling
T   ake the time to think of Baby Jesus
M ary and Joseph and the Holy Story
A   ll the Christians begin to celebrate
S   eeing happiness shed around the world.

Reuben Phillips (11)
Leopold Primary School

THE WITCH'S RECIPE

The moon is full,
We need a bull,
Chop it up and that is all,
Eye of newt
And something cute,
Oil, toil, boil and bubble,
I know someone's in trouble.
A dinosaur's bones and
Something a dragon owns.
Oil, toil, boil and bubble,
I know someone's in trouble,
Thrice blind mice,
Chopped twice,
All we need is a chopping knife.

Catrina Currie (10)
Leopold Primary School

NEIGHBOUR POEM

N   ice neighbour never neglect neighbour.
E   verybody eats everything.
I   nteresting imagination.
G   raceful garden.
H   en house.
B   lue boarder, bluebells.
O   utside orderly orchard.
U   nassuming understanding.
R   ather regal.

Wasim Bilal Parvez (11)
Leopold Primary School

MY FRIEND FRED

I have a friend called Fred
Who has the weirdest head.
He's got sticky-up hair
Like a prickly pear.
He's got big blue eyes
Like a buzzing fly's.
He's got a long sharp nose
Like a thorny rose.

He's got a great chin
Like a baked bean tin.
He's got sticky-out ears
Like jugs of beer.

Venezia Justinne Pitter (8)
Leopold Primary School

ENVIRONMENT

E veryone lives in an environment.
N one of them know the rule.
V ery often they destroy the town.
I gnore the town in every way, they don't
R ecognise that the government is watching.
O f course, they don't care if they are doing wrong
N obody has a reason to say something.
M oments fly as they think of the environment.
E ven if they see anyone doing anything
N one of the people say anything.
T alk about the environment. *Please!*

Grace Kiarie (9)
Leopold Primary School

THINGS FOUND IN A SCHOOL BAG

A   A half eaten juicy *a*pple
B   An ugly bouncy *b*all
C   A cool disco *c*alculator
D   A dirty toy *d*og
E   A rubber *e*lephant
F   A *f*ireman's bendy doll
G   A *G*oldilocks book
H   A handy *h*at
I   A block of *i*ce
J   A wobbly *j*elly
K   A funny *k*angaroo pencil top
L   An icky sticky *l*ollipop
M   A mad talking toy *m*onkey
N   A bendy *n*ail
O   A bean toy *o*ctopus
P   New pens and *p*encils
Q   A book on how to be a *q*ueen
R   A long folding *r*uler
S   A *s*tudying book
T   A freaky *t*elephone
U   An old brown *u*mbrella
V   An unbreakable plastic *v*ase
W   A *w*ildlife book
X   A *x*ylophone
Y   A *y*ellow gel pen
Z   A cool dude *z*ebra pencil case.

Marissa Ferguson (10)
Leopold Primary School

THINGS FOUND IN A SCHOOL BAG

A   Whole mouldy *a*pple
B   Big, flat *b*all
C   A new cool *c*alculator
D   A big bendy *d*og
E   A broken *e*gg holder
F   An old *f*ry-up
G   Dirty, mouldy *g*rapes
H   Dirty, messy pencil *h*older
I   *I* saw a dead frog in my bag
J   An ugly *J*apanese doll
K   A broken, bended *k*ite
L   A *l*ittle broken pencil
M   A little pretend *m*ouse
N   A soft *n*ice ball
O   A mouldy old *o*range
P   An old dirty *p*ig
Q   An old *q*ueen doll
R   A *r*usty pencil case
S   A slithering green *s*nake
T   The 'Boys *T*ale of Childhood' book
U   An *u*gly chicken found the day before
V   A *v*ery nice book
W   *W*e found our book
X   An *X*-men boy doll
Y   *Y*ou like a doll book
Z   A *z*ebra animal toy.

Laura Laville (10)
Leopold Primary School

BIRTHDAY HAIKU

Birthdays are good fun,
It's so hard when you prepare
And doing the plans.

Making and baking,
Writing the invitations,
Ready to post them.

Preparing the food
And finding entertainment,
The decorations.

Bring in the people,
Bring in the entertainment,
Get the food finished.

Presents coming here,
People saying, 'It's great fun,
Thank you very much.'

Ariel Lavonne McPherson (11)
Leopold Primary School

WHAT WILL WE BE?

Mummy, oh Mummy come with me,
You see what I will be,
Is it good or is it bad?
Hey, am I mad?

Mummy, oh Mummy,
What will you be?
I don't know, come and see,
Is that a bee? No it's me.

Now everybody knows what they will be,
Hold on, what will I be?
I don't know, come and see,
Wow! Is that me?

Does everybody know what they will be?
Yes we do,
Very good,
Hey, is Dad in the loo?

Reion Tibby (8)
Leopold Primary School

A POEM ABOUT POLLUTION

Mummy, oh Mummy, what is that pollution
That people are talking about?
Is it that banana skin
Or is it those cars that are smoking
Their fumes in the air?
Pollution spreads all about in the country.
It can be dangerous too.

Mummy, oh Mummy, who makes pollution?
Why don't they stop it, 'cause it's dangerous?
Don't people care about others?
They just don't think.

Mummy, oh Mummy, what's going to happen
If all that pollution goes on?
Will we be safe or will we die?
That cannot go on, it must stop!
Stop polluting our country.

William Musumba (8)
Leopold Primary School

FAVOURITES

Eyes, eyes,
They let you see,
You have to protect them
When you go swimming wear goggles,
Eyes, eyes.

Cars, cars,
They look all right,
My match is Mercedes,
They drive you mad, but I'm all right,
Cars, cars.

They shine
A ray of light,
Enters your eyes and shines
So you can definitely see,
Shine, shine.

Glow, glow,
In the dark,
Make sure you look nice
So you can look bright in the night,
Glow, glow.

Sparkle
In the dark night,
Sparkle.

Adiat Bashorun (11)
Leopold Primary School

THE CHASE RACE

In the race
We showed the pace
To run the chase
For the case

It was the chase
To tie the race
To pull up the case
Then that was the race.

Luke Anderson-Moore (9)
Leopold Primary School

SCHOOL IS FUN

School is fun,
Lots of friends,
Lots of teachers,
To teach new things.

We learn English,
Romeo and Juliet.
We learn maths,
$4^2 = 4 \text{x} 4$.
We learn science,
The heart pumps blood around.
We learn ICT,
The Internet has lots of search engines.
We also learn history,
Is it black history month?
We think of the past.
School, school, it's really fun.
We have lots of extra activities,
Like netball, football and hockey.
We play and we enjoy them.
I want to be a netball player.
Well, that is school for me,
But I hope your school life
Will be just as much fun as mine.
School is really fun!

Adetola Adefarasin (9)
Leopold Primary School

I CAN ACHIEVE

Do I have a skill?
I sometimes ask myself.
My mum says I have a skill,
But I need to achieve it.
But what is that skill?
I sometimes ask myself,
As I sit on my bed, I ask myself.
Is that skill being the best I can possibly be . . .
Or is it being someone grand?
Buying a house or zillion acres of land.
Maybe I can take out all the money from my bank
And give it to the poor?
Or give food to people that can't afford any?
Maybe I can try and be real smart
And try to give it to people who need it the most?
But I want to be someone famous, like Mother Theresa.
Now I have discovered my skill
And that's being as nice as I can possibly be.
I might be little now, but I can grow
And achieve my dream
And that's exactly what I am going to do.

Lavon Andrew-Bishop (10)
Leopold Primary School

A SORRY POEM

Sorry can mean anything
Sorry means not to be hurtful
Sorry means not to be mean
Sorry means to be truthful.

Sian Williamson (11)
Leopold Primary School

MY BROTHER AND SISTER

André, André, you're a naughty boy,
You shouldn't throw your food away,
Give it to Mum, she'll know what to do,
She eats her food every day.

Rose, Rose, you look nice,
You've got a colourful dress.
What are you doing? Why are you putting on your shoes?
Oh, that's a really big bruise.

André, André, do you want to go to the shop with me?
Wow, I think I'll get an ice lolly.
What do you want?
Oh! You want a lolly.

Rose, Rose, you're a naughty girl today.
Don't, don't hurt André.
Work together,
Play together,
Grow up together.

Jasmine Ellington (7)
Leopold Primary School

SAFETY

S   afety is a very important thing
A   nd if you don't be careful you could get hurt.
F   or all the things you should be thinking about, it should be safety.
E   lectricity is dangerous.
T   hink before you act.
Y   ou should always listen.

Jerome Best Peart (9)
Leopold Primary School

MY NAME IS CASSANDRA

My name is Cassandra
You can't date me
You can't date me
Cos I'm too pretty.

My name is Cassandra
I'm so cool
I'm so cool
I'll make you drool.

My name is Cassandra
You're so dry
You're so dry
All I say is, bye, bye, bye.

My name is Cassandra
You're not cool
You're just in Year 1 at school.

Cassandra Ashlee Parkes (9)
Leopold Primary School

DREAM

In a dream you can be a dragon,
Blowing fire through the night.
Or you could be a gladiator,
Having a vicious fight.

You can even be Craig David,
Singing all day long.
Or you can be a lion,
In a hot place where you belong.

If you want, you can be the queen,
Drinking from a fancy cup.
Then, all of a sudden,
You open your eyes and wake up.

Rommell Miller Bennett (10)
Leopold Primary School

THE CARIBBEAN

Sand golden
Glistening in the sun
Seashells of every shape and size
Calm sea
Calm waves
Children mucking about
Sandcastles in the sand
Ice cream stalls with different flavours
Bikinis, swimming costumes
All different colours
Umbrellas on shores
Buckets knocked over
Moats built around castles
Seaweed floating in the sea
Fishing boats on the horizon
Little houses made of straw
Nice sunsets
Souvenirs selling in little shops
The orange sunset sky.

I love the Caribbean.

Rochelle Hutchinson (9)
Leopold Primary School

ABOUT MY WEEK'S WEATHER

Sunday, warm and sunny,
A nice day to go out and eat some honey.

Monday is cold, cold, cold,
Mum says you have been told.

Tuesday burning hot,
Dad says go and visit Scot.

Wednesday spring,
Nice little bluebells sing.

Thursday snowy and blowing,
Throwing all balls are frosty.

Friday brings summer blazing in scent,
Sleeping eyes go too sleeping.

Saturday,
Darkest night ever.

Deandra Munroe (7)
Leopold Primary School

WATER

Water is fresh,
Water is cool,
Water is very nice in a big pool.

You can drink water,
You can sink in water,
That's why you never think.

Tajha Coleman-Ellis (8)
Leopold Primary School

WEATHER

Sunday, sunny, early morning,
Light in the evening.

Monday, cloudy in the morning,
Rainy in the evening.

Tuesday, I said hey . . .
After I ran away.

Wednesday, we play, play, play,
Till the end of the sun.

Thursday, rainy day,
So no play, play, play.

Friday, sunny day,
Plus the end of school for the week.

Saturday, really sunny day,
To do some shopping, to go to the beach.

Taalib Rowe (8)
Leopold Primary School

THE BEGGARS ARE COMING

Hark, hark,
The dogs do bark,
The beggars are coming to town,
Some in rags,
Some in Jags
And one in a velvet gown.

Alysia-Shai Keely (10)
Leopold Primary School

MOUNTAINS

Mountains huge, big, snowy,
Dangerous, scary, no way.
Don't go, please don't go, oh no!
Dangerous!

Lovely, happy not sad,
Sunny, cute, beautiful.
Not rocky, not bumpy, just smooth.
Mountains.

Some are rocky, bumpy, cute,
Some are nice, beautiful.
Some are dangerous, smooth,
I like mountains.

I know goats live on rocks,
People go travelling or hiking.
On snowy mountains they ski,
Fun mountains.

Sadia Latif (10)
Leopold Primary School

MY FAVOURITE GAMES

Lara Croft, Scooby-Doo,
My friends all have them too.
Resident Evil is the kind
That my action friend wouldn't mind.

My favourite is Max Payne,
Whilst Bugs Bunny is just insane!
Sim City is very cool
And WWE Smackdown also rules!

Harry Potter is great fun
And in Halo you get a gun.
Olympic Games are very tiring,
Whilst in Spider-Man I keep firing, firing, firing!

All these games are the best,
They aren't boring like the rest!

Dareon Hanlon (9)
Leopold Primary School

MY SCHOOL

My school
is really cool,
it's like a pool
and it hasn't a fool.

My school
is really cold
and very old,
it smells like mould.

My school
is very spacious
and is gracious,
we are conspicuous
and I am continuous.

My school
is really cool,
it's very old
and is gracious
and we all love it!

Valerie Amissah (10)
Leopold Primary School

NO MORE WARS

Just ten and still growing up,
All I hear is wars, hostility, fights.
I am scared if there is a chance for me
To grow up in peace and love.

There is love at home,
With parents, brothers and sisters.
But why is love lacking
Between countries, towns and villages?

The world needs love, peace and joy,
No more wars.
No more people carrying guns around the world.
People get shot, families get hurt.
Please stop the war.

Nathan Omar Gray (9)
Leopold Primary School

ELECTRICITY

When I put a plug into the wall,
It lights up all of my hall,
I could invite people to a ball,
Or maybe I could set up a stall,
In a multicoloured shopping mall.
I'm teaching you this
Because it's not a fuse,
So next time you touch it,
It will be full of use!

Haider Bashir (8)
Leopold Primary School

WATER HAIKU

Water can make floods,
Water is a nice, cool drink,
Water is very cool.

Water is used for so many things,
Water is really fun,
Water is used for rivers.

Water is very cool!
Water can be really dangerous,
In storms, wind and rain.

But all the time I must keep safe,
If I don't . . .
Coastguards will help me out!

Llimahl Okocha (9)
Leopold Primary School

MAKE LONDON SAFE

Help the children to have a better life,
Avoid the drugs, avoid the fear,
Realise what will happen in the future.
If we carry on like this,
Life should be happy, safe and sound.
Stop the shouting, stop the killing.
Everyone has to change from wrong to right,
Now keep London *safe!*
'Cause that's where we love to be.

Candice Falconer (9)
Leopold Primary School

MY FRIEND TED

I have a friend called Ted,
Who has a very big head.
He has very spiky hair,
Like a prickly pear.
He has very bendy knees,
Like very long peas.
He has dark brown eyes,
Like a bay horse's behind.
He has short, straight legs,
Like garden pegs.
He has extremely big ears,
Like strawberry pies,
But he will be my friend for evermore.

Kanyin Fagade (9)
Leopold Primary School

MY WATER POEM

Water, water can be fun,
Water, water can be dangerous,
When you're sitting in the sun
You see people on the run.
Don't be such a copycat,
Lifeguards will tell you,
'Don't do that.'

Tell your friends to tell your friends,
'Don't be such a copycat
A lifeguard will tell you that.'
So be safe, so be good
And don't be a copycat.

Domonique Smith (8)
Leopold Primary School

FOOTBALL CRAZY

Big and hard,
Round and bouncy,
Fly in the air, roll on the green grass,
Get kicked on the pitch,
Get kicked into the goal.
My colour - black or white makes no difference,
For all colours of people play with me.
Each day I get kicked on the pitch by children and adults.
People hit me,
They kick very hard.
They stamp on me,
Some even knee me and some head me.
What a life I have.
Though in pain,
I give joy to millions.

Matthew Kendall (10)
Leopold Primary School

THE SHIP

Extremely
  High wave
    Ship clashing
      People drowning
       Captain shouting
      Women
        Screaming
         Wood floating
        Children
        Crying.

Chezney Cassell (9)
Leopold Primary School

IF I WERE . . .

If I were an ant I would
Walk in herds all day and night
If I wanted to.

If I were a frog
I would hop around
All day.

If I were a dog
I would bark every day
And night.

If I were a cat
I would walk around
Every day and night.

If I were a fish
I would swim all day.

If I were a rat
I would look for cheese.

Lamar Charlemagne (8)
Leopold Primary School

IF I WERE

If I were a dog
I'd bark all day
And scavenge every day
In the night I would laugh in a way.

And my mother couldn't tell me
It's a wicked thing to do
Since she would be a dog
And she would do it too.

If I were a mouse
I'd nibble all day
And eat cheese for the rest of the day
If I had a cold I would say *eek*.

And my mother couldn't tell me
It's a wicked thing to do
Since she would be a mouse
And she would do it too.

Patrice King (8)
Leopold Primary School

MY FAVOURITE BOOKS

Books, books, books,
they help you with your education
and to make you read a lot better.

Some books are interesting, some are not,
it's better to read than to sit down at home
playing video games and eating popcorn all day.

Put the video games down,
switch off the TV,
go up to the shelf and read a book.

The books I like reading are:
Roald Dahl, 'Nicobobinus' and
'Why Shepherds Wash Their Socks'.

I really hope you read a lot of books,
because books will help you a lot
with things you need to do.

Antonia Jones (10)
Leopold Primary School

FOOTBALL SPEAKS

I am round, big or small
I get kicked against the wall.
I'm small to people
But I'm big to myself.
To me the children look like elves
But some look like giants.
I get kicked in the net
And people shout *hooray!*
I feel like I'm abused.
Each day I get thrown,
Headed, punched and kicked.
They don't feel my pain
It really, truly hurts.
But now I know
I'm just an old, playing
Football.

Rochelle Hylton (10)
Leopold Primary School

WATER

Water can be great,
Water can be bad,
You can die in water
And you can float in water.
Water can be great,
Water can be bad.

Terrisa Bennett (8)
Leopold Primary School

THE RIVER

Wet,
The river splashes,
The river gurgles,
The river ripples,
The river flows.
Wet,
The river's long,
The river's cold,
The river's blazing,
Oh, that's amazing.
Wet,
The river's got swans,
The river's got boats,
The river's got ducks,
What more can you say?

Daisy Luyiga (9)
Leopold Primary School

WHITE SNOW

As the hail drifts away,
I see a flake and white snow.
The snow falls onto the ground,
Children are glad to see it, they're very cheerful.
Snow puts a sparkle in children's eyes.
When the snow falls onto the ground,
Children always smile.

Chanté Burrows (9)
Leopold Primary School

WATER, WATER

Water! Water!
Is the best in the west!
Water! Water!
It can help you to have some fun!
Water! Water!
It is such fun and dumb!
Water! Water!
It is as numb as a plum!
Water! Water!
It is strong but it could be like a pond!
Water! Water!
You could splash, splash, all day!
Water! Water!
Is better than anything!

Kane Pfeiffer (9)
Leopold Primary School

ELECTRICITY

E stands for electricity, the most powerful thing.
L stands for learning a different language.
E stands for each other.
C stands for cars going round the curve.
T stands for telephones ringing all day long.
R stands for religious education.
I stands for ice cream.
C stands for crying.
I stands for I can think all day.
T stands for today.
Y stands for yoghurt.

Shaina Quaye-Iskander (8)
Leopold Primary School

WATER SAFETY

Be safe with water safety
Make sure you're dry
But if you're on a little rock
Just try and try and try.

Be safe with water safety
Make sure you're dry
Don't cry and cry and cry
Just try and try and try.

Be safe with water safety
Make sure you're dry
If you're stuck on a rock
Just wave your arms
And you might have some luck.

Oyinka Bolatiwa (8)
Leopold Primary School

I CAN DO IT AND ACHIEVE IF I BELIEVE IN MYSELF

I am determined to achieve,
I am also believing that I can achieve.
Each day I follow my dreams.
I can do it, I can do it.
And if I fail,
I will try harder.
I would achieve to be a doctor
Or a teacher.
Whatever I do,
I would remain with higher education.
I believe I can do it.

Nicole Mumuni (11)
Leopold Primary School

A POEM ABOUT POLLUTION

'Mummy, oh Mummy what is pollution?'
'Pollution is mess darling, dear Cherelle,'
'Mummy, oh Mummy do not drop litter there,
Chocolate paper and crisp packets.'

'Mummy, oh Mummy, what is that?'
'It's pollution again, pollution daughter
That is mess.'

'Mummy, oh Mummy do not drop anything,
'It's banana skins and cans and extras you're dropping.'

'Mummy, oh Mummy do not drop bubblegum and chewing gun,
It's pollution again, you're dropping.'

Mickaela Moore (7)
Leopold Primary School

THE RAIN

Umbrellas in the rain
Puddles everywhere
Pavements and roads wet
Everyone trying to stay warm
Sitting near the fireplace
Hot cup of tea
Cold, damp
Rain dripping
Rain rushing
Rain falling heavily
The rain.

Sarai Stern (10)
Leopold Primary School

SPLASH IN THE WATER

Water is fun to play in and splash in.
Water is best in the north-west.
Water is dangerous and spectacious.
Water is fake in a lake.
Water is like blood, but some people can flood.
Water is very bad, but some people are really sad.
Water is really rough, but something can get really tough.
Water is metallic like an attic.
Water is like a pond when you're showing your wand.
Water is smooth like a roof.
Water is bright in the night.
Water is loud when it goes around.

Nicole Murray (9)
Leopold Primary School

KEYS AND LOCKS

I am a brass lock,
I am a brass key.

I am a silver lock,
I am a silver key.

I am a gold lock,
I am a gold key.

I am a rusty lock,
I am a rusty key.

I am a door lock,
I am a door key.

Sherica Matthews (9)
Leopold Primary School

IF I WERE

If I were a cat,
I'd lick myself all day
And roll around on the floor
In a funny sort of way.

And my mother couldn't tell me,
It's a wicked thing to do,
Since she would be a cat
And she would do it too.

If I were a dog,
I'd chase cats all day
And eat my food
In a nasty sort of way.

And my mother couldn't tell me,
It's a wicked thing to do,
Since she would be a dog
And she would do it too.

If I were a rat,
I'd scamper around all day
And squeak a lot
In a neat sort of way.

And my mother couldn't tell me,
It's a wicked thing to do,
Since she would be a rat
And she would do it too.

Jhonelle Williams (8)
Leopold Primary School

THE BEACH

Rippling water
Yellow sand
Hot sun
No rain
Sandcastle
American flags
Blue sky
People swimming
Ice cream licking
Dogs chasing
Everyone to the beach.

Jonathan Williams (10)
Leopold Primary School

WHAT AM I?

Every time you feed it
It grows larger
And if you survive it
You'll be darker than ash
It will go out if you give it a drink
And die if not fed enough
Some of them are wild
But aren't welcomed
They ransack forests
And have no pity
They take out the weak
But don't attack water
What am I?

Fire.

Felix Cadieu (10)
Lyndhurst House School

THE TREE

Standing there looking around,
Its huge hand with long fingernails,
It has no clothes on except its skin,
No hair on its head,
Its leg's stuck to the ground,
Its eyes as holes wide open,
With no mouth to eat with
But a mouth to drink with,
Its hand swaying in the wind,
The sun shining at it,
The darkness creeping on it,
The moon high in the sky
Looking down on it.

Adam Gigi (10)
Lyndhurst House School

GOLDFISH

I am gold as a ring but not so small,
I have eyes shaped like a protractor,
I have fins like golden stars but not as big,
My body is small as a mouse,
I am scaly as a lizard and fast as a leopard,
My body is streamline like a seal,
I will not blink.

Guy Hayakawa (9)
Lyndhurst House School

THE PARROT

It glides in the air like a plane
Its colours are like a rainbow
Its wings are like soft leaves
Its beak is as sharp as a knife.

Its food is mice
It is silent like night
It lives in the jungle
And its eyes glow in the dark.

Sam Berrick (10)
Lyndhurst House School

HARRY THE HAMSTER

The ebony black fur with ivory-white mixed in
His little legs - cigarettes with paws
His teeth like little nail clippings, sharpened.
With eyes like small beetles
He runs around like a headless chicken
Then falls soundly asleep.

Hugo Woodhead (10)
Lyndhurst House School

SHARKS

Sharks glide in the water,
Like a plane in the air,
Only eating things in his way,
Never leaving things behind.

So many sharks in the water,
They are predators,
No one can stop them,
They are the masters of the sea.

The sharp diamond glides in the water,
Sharks have no mercy for others
And the fishes say
'I wish they weren't here.'

Lucien Cadieu (10)
Lyndhurst House School

THE TIGER

It silently walks across the planes,
With dashing hair all about
And its sharp teeth glistening in the sun
With its little pink snout.

The bruises on its fur
Orange, white and black
Dozing off in the sun
It is one of the cats.

As it steps quietly through brown bushes
Whilst it camouflages as well
Waiting for the time to pounce
Because it has good smell.

Now its day has come to an end
It has finished its prowl
I am going home right away
And the last thing I heard was a growl.

Tarik Basri (10)
Lyndhurst House School

PARROT

I am like a rainbow
Gliding through the sky
Full of many colours
And also I can fly.

I am a walkie talkie
Talking all day
And when night comes
My talking fades away.

My wings are like huge trees
All magnificent and bushy
Always bouncing up and down
Until I get snoozy.

Gregory Dagul (10)
Lyndhurst House School

PARROTS

There is a mighty waterfall
Where on cliffs there lies some birds
The parrot family gleaming brightly
Hovering in their pride.

The parrots are spectacular
Their eyes like big moons
Twinkling in the sun
They have curvy beaks, curly and neat
Their nostrils lay before.

Their wings are like fans
Which flap at mighty speed
The king parrot of the crowd,
Then takes the lead.

The feathers are multicoloured
From orange right down to blue
Some parrots go to find food.

The twilight soon arrives
The parrots start to sleep
For one place there was so much squawking,
There's not even a little peep.

Mark Mindel (10)
Lyndhurst House School

RUBBER DUCKIE

Bath day again!
Wet again!
What a bloomin' pain again!

Water running, glug, whiz,
What sort of torture is this?

Is my mother insane?
She could have punished me
A bit more humane.

The gushing stopped,
My heart sank,
I feel like a prisoner,
Walking the plank.

Splash, splosh in I go,
Is it horrible, mank and wet?
Just so!

I drop in bubble bath,
Dollop, splog, stick my
Hand up the tap,
Feels like bog.

I swill in there,
I can sneak out if I'm lucky.

Uh oh, here comes Mum
With my beloved rubber duckie.

She dunks him in,
Splatter, splatter,
Making all the
Bubbles scatter.

I pick up duckie
(His name is Chris)
Splash I'm quite
Enjoying this.

Five minutes chill,
Sat up, mind tranquil and still.

I like bath time to learn,
Splash out, little sister's turn.

Lily Aaronovitch (9)
New End Primary School

DEATH

Many wars have been fought
But none are much the same
Many wars I have fought
But none much the same
But one war, a very odd war
I was hit but I still live
I feel very light
When I look in the mirror
I am really quite pale
Everybody fails to see me
Nothing quite hurts me as much as it did before
I am quite a bit taller
Or I can be small
This life really is quite good.

Murtathe Jawad (10)
Oliver Goldsmith Primary School

THE LAST ALLIANCE

The orcs charge as the elves fire,
When hobbits sleep unaware in the shire,
The last alliance of elves and men
Knocking orcs down to ten but then
In his armour Sauron walked
His powerful mace as deadly as a hawk
He smashed through man's lines
Like water on rock,
Until Elendil the king of men
Thought that he must fight again,
He ran at Sauron, Narsil raised,
Until he was smashed by Sauron, that day.
Elendil dead, all hope was lost,
This death was a terrible loss.
His son Isildur took up his father's sword
And with one full swipe Sauron was never more.
The ring was now in Isildur's hands,
'Destroy it,' Elrond shouted the world's future in mind,
Isildur said 'No,' the typical man,
Weak with pride and power in hand.
Later that year Isildur fell
And now the story of the ring is hard to tell
Into the river Anduin the ring was lost
But then a hobbit found a ring
And oh what an amazing thing.

Nicholas Hurley (11)
Oliver Goldsmith Primary School

DOLPHIN

Loud splasher
High jumper

Fish eater
Tail swisher

Blue swimmer
Human watcher

My close friend
Dolphin.

Dinusha Moorthy (10)
Oliver Goldsmith Primary School

FUNNY PEOPLE

Every day when I'm going to school
I see people who look like fools,
I see people with weird school bags
And people telling unfunny gags.

Every day when I'm going home
I see people with afro combs,
I see people riding on tricycles
And funny headlines on the daily chronicles.

Every day when I'm going out
I see funny animals walking about,
But their owners seem to be even more mad
What's this world coming to? Isn't that bad?

Every day when I'm at school
I see this boy who's a real fool,
I won't say his name, it will embarrass him
But I tell you now he acts like a chimp.

Every night when I'm in bed
I think of the next day in my head,
My bunkbed sways and floorboards creek
But slowly, I fall asleep.

Jake Shuter-Ross (10)
Oliver Goldsmith Primary School

THE CASTLE

On the outside it is dark,
Very dark indeed,
I feel really scared,
Help is what I need.

The big brown doors are rusty,
Too rusty for me,
I am really shivering,
I want my mummy.

I open the big castle door,
With a lot of ease,
Now I feel really sick,
Help me, please!

The tower is flashing,
Who is it I see?
I'm a detective,
Do you want a piece of me?

The dungeon is full of skeletons,
That are so smelly,
I am going to throw up,
I can feel it in my belly.

The weapons' room is dangerous,
Cor blimey!
Did you see that arrow?
It went right through me.

The throne is sparkling,
Like a great ruby,
It is spotless,
I wish the king was me.

The gallery is full of paintings,
Of old kings and queens,
Wait a minute, who is that?
Is that a picture of me?

I can hear spooky noises,
Too spooky, help me!
I am swirling round and round and round,
. . . because it was a dream!

Nikos Yerolemou (10)
Oliver Goldsmith Primary School

DEATH

On the 31st of a ghastly May
Where my beloved grandad lay,
I mourned for happiness,
Death was to much for me, thus,
A dark spirit like nightfall,
The wind howling as it called
I glared at my grandad's face,
Between life and death on the chase,
It was like a devil killing,
Pouring, death, spilling,
I couldn't understand death,
It was too much for me,
I couldn't take it on, you see,
The problem is, I never knew him,
Only in my dream.

Amish Garala (11)
Oliver Goldsmith Primary School

HAUNTED HOUSE

A lovely new house, just for me,
I see it is daylight,
It looks grave at night,
Excited and happy, I stepped inside,
To find someone, just for me.

Screaming, crying all night long,
Never-ending, never stopping.

Two weeks later, screaming,
Pitiful crying, a horrid sound,
Nothing I've ever heard before,
It was coming from the bathroom,
It used to be a spare bedroom, so who was there?

Screaming, crying all night long,
Never-ending, never stopping.

No one was there,
What was going on?
A girl weeping all night long,
But things went further,
A crack in the kitchen, loud and menacing.

Screaming, crying all night long,
Never-ending, never stopping.

Food covered the floor,
I got scared, so I told my husband,
He didn't give a toss, said it was the dog,
I couldn't go to sleep for a week,
What was going on?

Screaming, crying all night long,
Never-ending, never stopping.

I was having a shower,
All alone, when my sixth sense jumped,
I grabbed a towel and jumped out,
Pulled back the curtains.
Argh!

Screaming, crying all night long,
Never-ending, never stopping.

I started to scream,
After seeing her face,
Screaming at me with blood on her hands
And pale like a stormy sky
Something had happened, this house was haunted.

Screaming, crying all night long,
Never-ending, never stopping.

Doing research, I found a poem,
It told me everything
The girl was Eloies,
She starved to death in the spare room,
Murdered she was. Murdered.

Amanda Isaac (11)
Oliver Goldsmith Primary School

KANGAROO

Bunny jumper
Pouch slimer
Power boxer
Street fighter
Baby holder
My best pet.

Dillan Hamarash (10)
Oliver Goldsmith Primary School

JUNK FOOD PARTY

Twenty tins of Mini Rolls,
Heaps of sweets, each filled in bowls,
Forty cans of fizzy pop,
Be very careful, they're filled to the top!

In the oven, the burgers go,
Any onions? I'm afraid not, no.
In the oven go the French fries,
I really hate these plastic ties!

In goes the pizza, sweetcorn and ham,
Why am I holding the strawberry jam?
Put the biscuits on a plate,
Why are all our guests really late?

Packets of crisps, piled in a heap,
They're here! I know it! I can hear the *beep-beep!*
They go to the sweets, in the bowls,
Pull some out, then shout, 'Hey, Mini Rolls!'

We sit at the table, waiting for the food,
In come the burgers, Mum's in a mood,
In comes the pizza, the golden-brown chips,
In the freezer, go the triple whips!

Everyone starts eating our delicious food,
Now Mum isn't even in a bad mood!
When we've all finished, we start up on the whips,
Someone isn't having one, 'cause they've left all their chips!

Alex Rozanski (9)
Oliver Goldsmith Primary School

GHOST SONG

The person came swishing,
Swishing along the moor,
Knocking on my window,
Waiting till I opened the door.

I opened the door,
There was no one there,
Although I could hear a voice saying,
'Hello, I'm here.'

'I'm here to take you with me,
I'm here to keep you safe,
Even when you're with me,
You can always keep your faith.'

I stood there in shock and wonder,
Listening to everything,
I couldn't believe my eyes,
What was this? What would this person bring?

I had a faint idea,
To who it was outside,
It was my late grandmother,
Dressed as a bride.

I got a phone call last night,
To say that my grandmother had died,
I was shocked, I was surprised,
She had risen from where she laid.

Simone Belgrave (11)
Oliver Goldsmith Primary School

MY NAN

I saw her every Sunday
And I loved her so much
The night I heard that she had gone
I cried myself to sleep.
To hear such awful news
I first thought it was a lie
All I did was cry and cry.
I wish I could have said goodbye
To see her lay there
As still as the trees on a summer's day
The last few days I saw her, she couldn't even talk
She was very, very ill
Probably because she smoked
I wish she was here!
I wish she was here!
I wish she was here!
I don't understand why she had to leave
If I could see her for just one moment
That would be a dream come true.

Shakera Conger-Thompson (10)
Oliver Goldsmith Primary School

WHEN I WAS A LITTLE GIRL

When I was a little girl,
I felt that I had nothing,
But it feels like
I do have everything.

Now I have lots of friends and other things too,
But having lots of friends,
Makes me feel happy.

Now, it feels that I have nothing,
But soon it will be back!

By leaving the school,
I have lost my friends,
I want them back,
By the end of the day.

Nabilo Adde (10)
Oliver Goldsmith Primary School

HALL OF POP

AJ, from the Backstreet Boys,
Is really funny and plays with toys
Ben, from A1
Is really cool and really fun.

Britney Spears, she hasn't got a group,
But stays alone and plays with a hoop,
Shaznay, from All Saints,
Works all the time and then paints.

Rich, from Five
Is OK and he's really alive
Lee, from Steps,
He is nice and I'm a Oliver Goldsmith rep.

Robbie Williams,
He's got lots of things and is worth millions,
Shane from Westlife is a real pain.

The hall of pop is the place to be
But before you go, meet me.

Chenaii Crooks (8)
Oliver Goldsmith Primary School

BODY PARTS AND WHAT THEY DO

My dad's nose is as long as a hose,
My mum's nose is as red as a rose,
My brother's arm is as wide as a farm
And the reason for this is . . .
Because of what they eat . . .
They eat
Pigs wigs', poses' toeses,
Powers' flowers, dogs' frogs,
Cats' flats, dogs' paws.

And the reason for that is . . .
Because of what they read

The cooks' books, the newspapers,
Poos papers, toilets, the magazines, super queens.
But what they are eating
Now is a
Fat
Glam
Lion.

Georgia Eracleous (9)
Oliver Goldsmith Primary School

THE DEATH

One week had gone,
Since my grandfather had died,
I was next to him crying,
It was the saddest day of my life,
I remember the time,
When I used to sleep in my bed
And my grandfather used to tell me stories.

I used to have,
The best times of my life with my grandfather,
I thought that I was,
The most unluckiest person in the world,
Then when my grandfather died,
I wasn't there with him,
But I still remember him.

Amaan Hussain (11)
Oliver Goldsmith Primary School

THE FUSSY CAT AND THE LONESOME BIRD

The cat, the cat,
The fussy, fast cat,
She slowly creeps after her prey, as she cleans herself night and day.

The bird, the bird,
The sad lonesome bird,
She toddles sadly with no friends, while she thinks in her head her
world's going to end.

The cat, the cat,
Stops in guiltiness,
'Why all this crying and tears?'

The bird, the bird,
Stops to answer,
'It's because I have got no friends and no one cares.'

The cat, the cat,
Thought about that,
I've got no friends, so be my friend
So they lived happily ever after.

Safia Sagalar (9)
Oliver Goldsmith Primary School

RIDDLE

I'm blue
I cover one third of the world's population,
I'm drinkable,
Some of me is salty!

You can swim in me,
I'm lovely to see,
On a sunny day in Crete!

I'm natural,
I'm swimable,
You're sinkable,
In me!

I'm in a pool,
I look like drool,
What am I?

Water.

Adam Ali (10)
Oliver Goldsmith Primary School

THE WINDY TREES

The trees were shaking round and round
I couldn't help but listen to that windy sound
So I went outside and put on my jacket
But I still hear that awful racket.

I go back in, still I hear,
That awful sound still hurts my ear,
The wind blowing to the left that I chase,
I realise a speck of dirt in my face.

And then it was bedtime, very boring,
I couldn't wait for the sun to spit morning,
The trees were not windy - what a relief,
Because those trees gave me so much grief.

What was done, was done, these trees were cruel,
I couldn't catch some of the morning drool,
Then it just started to rain
I felt like I'll never go outside again.

Suuna Muganga (10)
Oliver Goldsmith Primary School

MY WINDY DAY

I went out of the house
Suddenly I got scared by a mouse
I walked up the hill
I felt a chill
Soon there was a breeze
It made me sneeze
I felt a shiver
It made me quiver
The wind was cold
It all seemed bold
Then I started to shake
When I heard a car brake
Is the wind blowing?
Yes, the birds are flying
I thought it was May
What a windy day!

Jasmine Agyekum (8)
Oliver Goldsmith Primary School

THE FANTASTIC SEA

The sea is a place to be
Lots of fishes, fantasies to see,
Waves swaying side to side,
Would be nice to ride and ride.

Whales splashing water everywhere,
Dolphins jumping here and there,
Nothing like the sea,
It's a lovely place to be.

Sharks roaring in the sea,
I wouldn't want to be someone's tea,
Stingrays lying on the sandy floor,
It makes me want to know more and more.

Jellyfish floating in the sea,
Octopus' tentacles eight to see,
Crabs clanking very loud,
Lobsters clicking very loud sounds.

The sea is the place to be,
Just come to the sea
And play with me.

Nathanael Wong (8)
Oliver Goldsmith Primary School

ALIEN CONVERSATION

'Hello, is this Rod?'
'Yeah, hello Joyn so how was your journey to Earth?'
'No, not that good they all fainted when they saw me.'
'Ah yeah, I know what you mean, so did they feed you?'
'Yeah kind of, they threw fruit and cabbages at me,'
'Was there any excitement?'

'Those humans got these cars with flashing lights,
I wonder what they were. Then they followed me,
I walked two steps and they were holding these
Metal sticks! I wonder what they wanted?
It's good we don't live on Earth!'

Jamie Helps (9)
Oliver Goldsmith Primary School

SOUNDS AND SIGHTS OF THE JUNGLE

Trudging through the uncut grass,
A howl and growl as I pass,
Beyond my ever wildest dreams,
A fuzz and blur is all it seems.

Butterflies flutter here and there,
Displaying magical colours everywhere,
Giant trees tower over me,
A monkey, a bug are many I see.

Parrots squawking extremely loud,
Not a single, fluffy cloud,
Tigers prowling around the shrubs,
Look closely to find many kinds of grubs.

Monkeys swing from tree to tree,
Exhibiting tricks for us to see,
Elephants trumpeting blaring sounds,
Extraordinary animals and plants can be found.

The jungle is the place to be,
Full of nature's beauties to see.

Niran Yoganayagam (8)
Oliver Goldsmith Primary School

THE GHOST

He was walking home on a dull winter's evening
Past the park, till he saw something, lurking in the forbidden graveyard
A shadow, a shadow in the graveyard
He crept in, into the deep, spooky graveyard.

He followed the shadow, past rows and rows of tombstones,
He tripped . . . Arghh! . . . over a tombstone,
He had tripped over Jack Swallbie's grave
He shrieked . . . he is Jack Swallbie.

He read the date - Born 1982 Died 1986
'I . . .I'm a . . . ghost!' He whispered sadly
He rubbed his hand over the dates
He had read it wrong - Born 1882 Died 1886.

'Phew!' he breathed. 'Probably someone else.'
By now he had lost sight of the ghost
Suddenly, something tapped his cold shoulder
He turned round slowly, nobody there.

He started to walk slowly, until he saw a figure
He threw a rock at it . . . it went straight through him,
Jack turned around and ran, ran as fast as he could
Ran out of the graveyard and onto the road.

He walked home slowly, at a snail's pace
He was never going back to the graveyard
Because all he knew
Was that something was in there.

He wanted to tell someone about his unpleasant experiences,
But he knew that nobody would believe him
So he decided to stay quiet
Of what he saw in the spooky, ghostly graveyard.

Kunal Mistry (10)
Oliver Goldsmith Primary School

TIGER

The tiger hid in the shade of the grass
Ready to pounce to feast at last
The antelope was eating not a worry in the world
Her child was quick, she was slow and old
The tiger chose his moment, perfectly timed,
He jumped on his prey, one thought in his mind
He ripped her open, her child ran
Tiger didn't care he'd got his dinner
The child had escaped, but tiger was still the winner.

Soon the pack joined him too,
They'd been watching the whole way through
They were happy for a bit
But then, man came, rifles raised
Wanting the striped skin to sell back home
The pack took off, at the sound of a bullet
One tiger hit, the bullet right in
The tiger killed was the hunter of the pack
Man was ready it was time to act.

Back home in England money was made
The tiger had been skinned everywhere
The men wanted more, more tigers dead
Maybe soon there'll be none left
This isn't right, why don't they kill us
Tigers shouldn't die for their skin
Let them live, let them be
They are animals just like us
Let them be free, let them be free.

Giovanni Pilides (10)
Oliver Goldsmith Primary School

THE HILLBILLY HIGH ROAD

Once in a village in Tennessee
There lived 100,000 hillbillies,
They all lived on High Road 71
And they all had giant shotguns,
I'll name you some of the hillbillies,
Yeah, I'll name you some, I'll name you three,
The Dumb Brothers and Tommy T.

The rest I can't remember,
Because they were born in September,
I'll name you some things they eat,
Bats' wings and lizards' feet,
100-year-old eggs
And people's heads,
Eye of newt and wing of bird,
Now Hillbilly High Road has turned into witch world.

Ibrahim Bah (9)
Oliver Goldsmith Primary School

RIDDLE

It has 15cm long teeth,
It has a small tail,
It has a hunch back,
When it sits down,
It hunts big animals,
It has lived for 6000 years,
It's from a cat family,
It's a s. . .

Humza Shahid (9)
Oliver Goldsmith Primary School

WHAT AM I?

I have a yellow skin
And brown spots.

I am very tall
And can reach trees.

I'm in a sandy place
I live in Africa.

Do you know me?
Who am I?
I am . . .

Giraffe.

Vithya Kankeyan (9)
Oliver Goldsmith Primary School

MY LIFE SO FAR

When I was zero I felt like a hero,
When I was one my life had begun,
When I was two I learnt to sit on the loo,
When I was three I learnt to spell wee
When I was four I learnt to say more,
When I was five I felt so alive
When I was six I played with some sticks,
When I was seven I felt as if I were in Heaven,
When I was eight I learnt how to skate,
When I was nine I felt pretty fine
When I was ten I used a big pen
Now I am eleven I named myself Devon.

Jamal Faizi (11)
Oliver Goldsmith Primary School

WHAT'S ON THE MENU FOR TONIGHT?

I've got jelly on the plate
From the wobbly state.

I've got tomato juice
With apricot mousse.

I've got sugar bugs
From honey tubs.

I've got vanilla snake
With a flick of a cake.

So that's what's on the menu tonight?

Just one more thing,
Is your belly all right?

Tolu Sehindemi (9)
Oliver Goldsmith Primary School

CONSOLES

I have a station
And I took it to the game station,
I had to get some games
So I bought some flame games,
My mum and dad were shamed
So I was the same
The games were lame
So I changed it for another game,
What am I?

Danny Castle (9)
Oliver Goldsmith Primary School

MY NAN
(In loving memory of Molly Nicholson)

I sat with her nearly every day,
But then that day finally came,
It wasn't fair for my nan to die,
I didn't cry, but I don't know why?
There every day she lay in that hospital bed,
I still can't get the thought into my head.

She didn't die of natural causes,
I was with her when she had her stroke,
It made me want to cough and choke,
The day of the funeral came at last,
It hurt me, I wanted it all to pass,
I needed to cry, tears wouldn't run down my face
I can still see them bringing in the coffin case.

It lay there right in front of me,
My mum got up and said her speech,
She started to cry
And that was how my nan died.

Danielle Hoo-Hing (11)
Oliver Goldsmith Primary School

THE GREEDY WOLF

There was a young wolf from the forest,
Who ate the campers porridge and
Fell asleep in the middle of the porridge.
He woke up in a terrible fright.

Robert Pflaumer (8)
Rainbow Montessori School

HALLOWE'EN

Hallowe'en is a very spooky night,
We all celebrate it and enjoy it,
When we go trick or treating, we dress up,
As witches, ghosts, pumpkins, devils and bats.
We all celebrate Hallowe'en at night,
We love eating food that looks disgusting.
Like worms, spaghetti and eyeball jelly
And don't forget to have witch's fingers
And we like drinking goblin blood-like juice
And we can have as many sweets as we like
And my best sweetie is sugary sweets,
It's bedtime we all have to go to bed
And if you are scared, check under your bed
But I'm sure there won't be any monsters.

Hana Fujimoto (9)
Rainbow Montessori School

THE CENTAUR

Older than the oak,
Guardian of the woods,
His beard is long and white
And his eyes like stars at night.

Half horse, half man,
His hand crisped on his bow,
Day by day, following the flow
Of the days that come and go.

Bart Sibaud (11)
Rainbow Montessori School

AUTUMN

While walking back through shiny golden leaves,
A magnificent stag appeared in view.
We stood and admired him through wooded trees,
The stag was camouflaged by autumn hue.
Crunching leaves beneath our feet startled him,
He leapt away through shafts of silver sun.
Back to the safety of the trees so dim,
We continued our walk feeling struck dumb.
When nearing the sea we heard crashing waves,
On reaching the sand crisp wind hit our cheeks.
We hid for protection in white sand caves,
But could not escape getting wet when in reach.
After much fun, we went back to our camp
And ate a hot meal feeling slightly damp!

Lily Thompson (9)
Rainbow Montessori School

MOON

The moon shining bright not always at night,
Grey, silver, blue all the colour for you.
Half moon, full moon, total eclipse doesn't matter which,
I like it when it's a half moon because I know it will be full soon.
When I look at the moon I can whistle a happy tune
I wonder if loons like to sit on the moon
If I could fly I would fly up to the moon,
I wonder if bats like to go up there too,
Man on the moon, please tell me that I can come up there too!

Vika Silvester (11)
Rainbow Montessori School

WAVING FLOWERS

In a beautiful garden far away,
There are waving flowers,
The sun warms them,
They look so, so beautiful.

Angelica Conner (8)
Rainbow Montessori School

ASLEEP BY THE TREE

Asleep by the tree
All you can hear
Is what is near.

Asleep by the tree
All you can see
Is your deep blue sea.

Asleep by the tree
The animals are meeting
While the carnivores are eating.

Dominic Boren (10)
Rainbow Montessori School

THE SUMMER HAIKU

Sun shines in summer,
Great time for a holiday,
Where should we go to?

Matija Milovanovic (9)
Rainbow Montessori School

REPTILES

Slimy frogs, scaly crocodiles,
Slithery snakes and sticky snails,
All reptiles in a row,
Always in the sun, never in the snow,
The jungle is green and the crocodiles look mean.

Charles Farley (8)
Rainbow Montessori School

TEA BY THE RIVER

Down by the river, I eat chopped liver for tea
And what do I see, I see a bird in a tree,
I thought and I thought and I guessed it was
A parrot while nibbling a carrot.

Down by the river, I ate and looked across the river
And saw a tiny gate and behind it was a garden
Full of flowers and at the other side,
Men were singing in some showers.

Alex Madden (11)
Rainbow Montessori School

RABBIT FROM YORKSHIRE

There was once a young rabbit from Yorkshire,
He thought he could conquer his land,
He jumped out of his cage,
Tripped on the rail, stepped on his tail
And landed in a bush!

Marianne Sibaud (9)
Rainbow Montessori School

HALLOWE'EN

Monsters and goblins, bats and skeletons,
Ugly monsters, slimy ghouls and more,
Vampires coming out of their coffins,
Witches on broomsticks with their black cats,
Ruthless demons and magical wizards,
Mummified mummies with evil zombies,
Spooky ghosts haunt the misty graveyard - *Boooo!*
Trick or treat, smell my feet, give me a treat,
Sculptured pumpkins with their glowing faces,
Dark windy weather makes the night scary,
Children dress up in costumes and masks,
Scary and frightening but fun too!

Jacob Farley (10)
Rainbow Montessori School

FOOTBALL

I am football crazy
I am football mad
I love football so much
Better than all the other lads!
I support Gunners
Because they're the best!
Man Utd are so bad
They can't even beat the old west!
I'm football crazy
I'm football mad
And I'll support the Gunners
Through good and bad.

Gregory Tuka (10)
St Agnes Primary School

AUTUMN'S BEAUTY

As autumn draws in,
Leaves float in the air,
Landing on the dirt,
Dustbins and pavements,
As the wind blows,
They tumble down
And get swept away,
By the cooling breeze,
They're rustling down,
These colourful leaves,
Like rainbow colours,
As light as feathers,
Shining in the golden sun,
Glistening for everyone.

Andreas Eleftheriou (11)
St Agnes Primary School

WEREWOLF

Scott woke up in the middle of the night,
A blood-curdling scream had gave him a fright,
Slowly but surely he crept out of bed
And onto the door, he was placing his head,
When all of a sudden in stormed the creature,
With dripping red teeth, a horrible feature.
Then the creature opened its mouth wide,
Chopped up the boy and threw him inside,
The beast crawled back into its den,
Scott never saw daylight ever again.

Ryan O'Riordan (10)
St Agnes Primary School

The Pied Piper Poem

Zip, zap, zip, zap,
   That's how the flute sounded.
Zip, zap, zip, zap,
   That's how the piper's lips rounded.
Zip, zap, zip, zap,
   That's how he grouped the children.
Zip, zap, zip, zap,
   That's how they got trapped.
Zip, zap, zip, zap,
   But two lame boys got away.
Zip, zap, zip, zap,
   And told the story far away!
          Zip, zap, zip, zap,
          Zip, zap, zip, zap,

Timothy Corkery & Daniel Clark (10)
St Agnes Primary School

Autumn

Autumn, autumn, falling leaves,
Roses dying, apples tumbling,
Leaves swaying in the breeze,
Conkers covering the ground,
Children rummaging around,
Roses dying, apples tumbling,
Days get shorter,
Wind starts to blow,
Soon there will be cold and snow.

Odera Mbadiew (10)
St Agnes Primary School

YEAR SIX MADNESS

Teachers yelling
Children stressed
SATs are drawing near
Will we pass or not?
The question is full of fear
Friends begin to split up
I feel like smashing the
Headteacher's coffee cup!
Teachers nag us to learn, learn, learn,
I feel my head is going to burn, burn, burn!
Parents at us all the time
Booster this, booster that
Level 4. Level 5,
Is it necessary to survive?
Secondary tests and interviews
Nervous, worried and shy.
Will we be accepted or rejected?
But when it's all over . . . yahoo!
It's been an irritating year
A nerve wrecking year,
A stressful year!
Now everything is calm and clear
Our journey to the Isle of Wight
Is now coming into sight!
Everyone will be delighted in the sun
Now *finally*
We'll have some fun!

Olenka Hrynchak (10)
St Agnes Primary School

THE KING OF PRETZEL LAND

The king of Pretzel Land
Had a pair of scary eyes.
He decided to snorkel to Rumpus Land
To find a suit his size.

He saw a kangaroo on its head
And there are flying monkeys around.
He saw people with five heads
Who live underground.

He gets some stinky mail.
He bought a pet elephant.
The elephant was tiny,
As small as a little ant.

He decided to go back
'Cause he hated to be walked by dogs.
He said goodbye to his friends
And he threw some logs.

Jessica Nock (8)
St Agnes Primary School

THE KING OF RAINBOW ISLAND

The king of Rainbow Island
Had quite colourful hair
He decided to skip to Future Land
To find a colourful pear.

The people were standing on their heads
The cats were flying in mid air
The monsters with ten eyes are crazy
And the dogs have loads of pink hair.

So the king of Rainbow Island
Went to a robot of Future Land
'Can I have one of your pears?
And then I'll give you a grand.'

So the king of Rainbow Island
Decided to skip home
And when he was halfway there
He decided to go to Rome.

Stefano Massaro (8)
St Agnes Primary School

THE KING OF CARTOON ISLAND

The king of Cartoon Island
Had a cartoony house.
He decided to fly to Ninja Island
To find a ninja mouse.

The king flew to Ninja Island
And saw the cookie sun
The king saw the doughnut river
And the king took a gun.

The king decided to try things
He ate the cookie sun.
He sailed on the dead Ninja river
But he didn't have any fun.

The king wanted to go home
And he had one nasty crash.
He hated the dead Ninja river
And he flew off in a flash.

Simon Abaigbe (8)
St Agnes Primary School

THE KING OF TOWER ISLAND

The king of Tower Island
Had a pair of talking feet
He decided to fly on an eagle
To find a bag of wheat.

So he saw some flying doughnuts
And ate lots of chocolate ants.
He yelled at the cheese people,
'Please don't eat my pants!'

He looked up at the black moon
He saw a big hexagon,
An ostrich was doing a funny dance
And so was a pink salmon.

He decided to fly on an eagle
Back to wacky home
The trees were too noisy
And he saw a funny gnome.

Amy McLaughlin (8)
St Agnes Primary School

THE KING OF THE SPOOKY ISLAND

The king of the spooky island
Had a strange mind
He decided to fly to the weird land
He wondered what he would find.

He was a flying doughnut
With two big heads.
It was raining cats and dogs
He needed to hide in a shed.

So he looked up at the sky
Right up to the big green moon
He saw a comet crushing
He saw a flying baboon.

He decided to jump back home
On a blue kangaroo
It jumped high in the sky
And the king said, 'Boo, hoo!'

Bernadette Sayers
St Agnes Primary School

THE KING OF SPOOKY ISLAND

The king of Spooky Island
Had a stinky bag of ice.
He decided to fly to Crazy Land
To find out if they're nice.

He went on flying doughnuts
And it was raining cats and dogs
As heavy as an elephant
And he saw some floating logs.

He went to look at the blue moon
And talked to the lion too
And when he was not looking
A jumping monkey said, 'Boo!'

The king of Spooky Island
Decided to fly back
Because the big blue moon
Was about to throw a sack.

Faye Robinson (8)
St Agnes Primary School

SKYSCRAPERS

How
tall
those
big
buildings
stood,
a
shame
they
got
knocked
down.
On
that
tragic
day
it
really
scared
the
town.

How
many
floors
those
buildings
had
nobody
knows,
it
just
makes
you
think
you're
lucky
to
have
your
toes.

Some
people
are
lucky
to
have
escaped,
that
tragic
day
will
never
be
forgotten
on
September
the
11th.

Kirsty Hardy (8) & Siobhan Cloran (9)
St Agnes Primary School

THE SEA

The sea brushes over barnacles,
bubbling and buckling in the springtime breeze.

The sea spreads across the sunset;
shrinks and sparkles under a bright summer sun.

The sea patrols over places,
pimpling and prickling on damp autumn days.

The sea angrily roars across the raging, rising rocks,
rejecting and raving when winter winds blow.

Erin Allen (10)
St Agnes Primary School

I AM...

I am a girl who is going to be a famous artist.
I wonder if I will ever go on an aeroplane.
I hear the raindrops falling on my head.
I see the clocks ticking every hour.
I want world peace!
I am a girl who is going to be a famous artist.

I pretend that the sky is candy.
I feel my mum's coat when I am sad.
I touch the ground when I walk.
I worry when I am lost.
I cry when I worry about my mum.
I am a girl who is going to be a famous artist.

I understand that I can't have everything I want.
I say, 'Help me to learn.'
I dream that one day I will get a bike.
I try to do my very best.
I hope that one day they will stop the war.
I am a girl who is going to be a famous artist.

Louise Russell (7)
St Agnes Primary School

An Alphabet Poem

A is for Anna who is very quiet and cute.
B is for a blue car which hoots and hoots.
C is for cat who sleeps all day.
D is for documents which you have to pay.
E is for Eddie who has lots of gorgeous sweets.
F is for Fred who stays in bed with warm sheets.
G is for giraffe who is very long and lanky.
H is for hanky which is very dirty and manky.
I is for ice cream which is very cold.
J is for jelly which was all sold.
K is for kangaroo who jumps really high.
L is for Louis who looks up at the sky.
M is for mum who is very kind and nice.
N is for naughty, sneaky mice.
O is for octopus who has eight legs.
P is for pyjamas which we hang out on the line with pegs.
Q is for queen who rules the world.
R is for Rita whose hair is curled.
S is for swings which girls and boys enjoy.
T is for Tara who plays with her toys.
U is for umbrella which stops you from getting wet.
V is for Vera who has a pet.
W is for wheel which goes round and round.
X is for X-ray that makes a sound.
Y is for Yorig who eats lots of buns.
Z is for zoom baby that always runs.

Laura Tyther (9)
St Agnes Primary School

An Alphabet Poem

A is for Anita who always kicks
B is for Ben who makes good tricks.
C is for Chris who's not very nice.
D is for Daniel who likes to play with mice.
E is for Edward who likes to kiss girls.
F is for Faye who eats cinnamon swirls.
G is for Grace who is very moody.
H is for Harry who's a goody-goody.
I is for Isabelle who is joyful.
J is for Jo whose behaviour is awful.
K is for Kirsty who's really kind.
L is for Louise who has a good mind.
M is for May who loves Love Hearts.
N is for Nana who likes curls
O is for Olivia who is really sweet.
P is for Peter who likes to eat meat.
Q is for Queen who is strong.
R is for Rachel who is long.
S is for Susanna who is tall.
T is for Tanya who is small
U is for Ulrika who is always happy.
V is for Victor who wears a nappy.
W is for Wayne who is mostly mad.
X is for Xavier who is sad.
Y is for Yong who is a pain in the back.
Z is for Zeno whose best friend is Zak.

Louise Gillian Condon (8)
St Agnes Primary School

THE KING FROM SIMPON ISLAND

The king from Simpon Island
Had a pair of smelly pants
He decided to catch a pizza whale
To find an enormousant.

He was going to Crazy Island
But he did not know the way
Finally he did get there
But he got there in late May.

You'll never guess what he had,
He had a chocolate house
And it was very sickening
It came with a small mouse!

When he got back home
He finally realised
He was eating chocolate
With some very cool guys.

Tom Hand (8)
St Agnes Primary School

SEA SEASONS

The summer's salty sea breeze spraying up the side of rocks,
swishing and swaying in the strong summer sun.

The winter sea rushes through the ragged rocks,
rocking rapidly among the sea's rowdy rocks.

Isabel Foulsham (9)
St Agnes Primary School

AN ANIMAL POEM

A is for alligator, who's got great big jaws,
B is for bear, who's got giant claws.
C is for crow, who's as black as night.
D is for deer, who leaps like a fright.
E is for emu, who lays great big eggs,
F is for ferret, who sleeps in soil beds.
G is for giant tortoise, who's got big feet,
H is for howling monkey, whose branches he leaps.
I is for iguana, whose scales are rock-hard,
J is for jaguar who catches his prey off guard.
K is for kestrel who nods his head real slow,
L is for lizard who is always full of woe.

Jasmin Carmel (9)
St Agnes Primary School

FOOTBALL CRAZY

I'm football crazy, I'm football mad.
I enjoy football so much that I'm better than that lad.

I support Arsenal because they're the best.
They're so good that they beat the rest.

I support the Gunners because they're so good
They always score when they should.

Red is the colour
Football is the game
Because Arsenal is the greatest name.

Dario Dorado (10)
St Agnes Primary School

SNOW AT SCHOOL

Swaying like a star,
Falling,
Twirling,
Dancing like a ballerina,
Gliding,
Twisting like a tornado,
Fluttering,
Flying like a plane,
Swirling like a snowflake.
Snow.

Philip Bosah (11)
St Agnes Primary School

SNOW POEM

I stared up at the purple and pink sky,
when the first snowflake twisted by.
Then another coiled to the ground,
without a sound they tumbled down.
I trudged along in the soft, white snow,
while it was still bleak and low.
The snow on the ground was a book telling a story,
using all footprints as words
and not a sound was heard.
Trees catching snowflakes as they spun down,
now encrusted like a crown.
Finally the last snowflake fluttered by
and the stars glided away from the sky.

Emily Johnson (11)
St Christina's School, St John's Wood

SNOW

As I gazed outside at the bleak white snow,
Snowflakes swirled all in a row.
The snow lay undisturbed,
Gleaming white without being heard.
Children laughing on their sleighs,
It was as if the snow was gleaming
In the sun's faint rays.
Trees were swaying with the weight of snow,
The babbling brook had seized to flow.
Branches captured snow in their leaves,
In the woods a badger heaves
Her young out of her blocked up hole,
Against the white she's as black as coal.
Happiness is in the air
And snow is flying everywhere.

Alexandra Thompson (10)
St Christina's School, St John's Wood

SNOW POEM

As glistening, fluffy snow sprinkles down so new,
the gleaming, peaceful atmosphere fills the tranquil view.

Children's shouts and laughs surround the snow
as they tumble, spin and twirl,
on their sledges they come to an end
as they lie on the snow and curl.

Pristine clean images fill a person's mind
as they stare at soft snow that is definitely one of a kind.

Noora Aboukhater (10)
St Christina's School, St John's Wood

COLONEL FROST

An army of soldiers storming down
Spurring faces with burning cold.
Colonel Frost at their helm
Fighting a battle of old.

They flashed their ice sabres
Wearing armour of white,
They flurried and fought
All through the night.

But then rose the sun
The battle was lost.
One man escaped;
Colonel Frost.

This battle is fought every blizzardy day
The soldiers fight on with out fear
They will never win because when the sun rises
All the soldiers will . . . disappear!

Francesca Goodway (10)
St Christina's School, St John's Wood

WINTER WONDERLAND

Untouched and silent
the winter wonderland lay
deserted not violent
and the light was at bay.

The swirling, curling
dove-white snow
the people murmuring
full of glow.

The trees had frozen,
icicles were thick,
the winter had chosen
our land to be picked.

Sabina Assan (11)
St Christina's School, St John's Wood

INDIVIDUALITY

I've always had confidence in my life
And I never had the burdens of strife.
But now I've learned to respect people whose lives have this effect
My recent experiences have led me to believe
It won't always be compliment I receive
That's why this poem is about individuality!
That what's in a person's soul is quality not quantity!
We each have a flicker of the Lord's love in us
And when we learn to nourish and coax it out
We can overcome the speed of any bus!
We can flit, fly and glide
And broaden our horizon's far and wide
We are all unique and special
We all add good traits to the world.
We all give a special aspect
We must have faith and stamina when criticism is being hurled
We must believe in ourselves and others!
Have great faith in their ideas and not stamp them into smothers!
Our individuality will take us far with it
We must stand proud and know we don't have to follow the crowd.

Izzy Francke (10)
St Christina's School, St John's Wood

SNOW POEM

The temperature falls to 0 degrees.
Frost is covering grass and trees.
Light is growing dim and night descends
Everyone knows the day has come to an end.
Impatiently children wait for snow that never seems to come.
Ticks from the clock seem like slow beats of a drum.
Finally the sky opens up to release
A mass of floating, drifting, whirling white.
Everyone knows the flakes will continue to sprinkle all night.
The light cascade of snow turns into sleet and hail
A gentle winter breeze has turned into a monstrous dangerous gale.
In the morning the wind ceased
And in the snow there did not appear to be a single crease.
The sun comes out and shows its dazzling rays,
With snow covering the ground the world seemed to be a maze.
The ground heats up and sharp icicles and splinters of snow
Turn to slush.
Children's dreams were stamped on, broken and crushed.
Snow oozes out of every corner
And all that remains are puddles of dirty water.

Camilla Turner (11)
St Christina's School, St John's Wood

SNOW!

Swirling snowflakes cascade to the ground,
making not the slightest sound.
Streets and roads are completely filled
with blankets of snow and the air is chilled.

As the temperature drops many degrees,
lakes and ponds begin to freeze.
While birds try to fly away,
branches on trees start to sway.

When the sun rises into the sky,
children and adults start to walk by,
chatting about the frosty weather,
that has never been any better.

Laura Fabris (11)
St Christina's School, St John's Wood

SNOW POEM

Dove-white flakes drift and swirl down,
a soft blanket of snow.
Peace fills the town.
Snow awakens from its gown,
the pristine, untouched sheet of snow
is crushed and disturbed.

First footsteps appear
the big blanket is ripped,
on the lane there is a passing deer,
its feet have completely lost their grip.
Its antlers rise, it listens for sound,
there is nothing but the crunching
of its feet on the ground.

Dawn creeps in and faces fill with joy.
People and children are breathless.
Snow attracts every girl and boy.
Children become restless.
Sleighs are brought out,
People ski,
'Hooray!' even the adults shout.
Everyone can see,
what snow is all about.

Marta Zwierzynska (10)
St Christina's School, St John's Wood

A Snow Poem

Arising from my bed, I was surrounded by trees,
teeming with picturesque snow.

Serenity of snow made it silent.
Fading moonlight made it twinkle.

A view like an isolated blanket, with no deep footsteps,
which made it unique.

Pristine as a new sheet,
just taken off a washing line.

A cold, bitter night which produced frost
on the stiff and frozen stream.
Opposite, a hill with fresh snow laid upon it.

Ever so slightly, bundles of snow
came drifting down below with twinkling snow.

Anna McEvoy (11)
St Christina's School, St John's Wood

Snow

Oozing slush, not even snow
tumbles down below.
Like a glance of mist
but thicker to the touch.
Snow, snow, snow,
on trees and rooftops it's all around
no matter what or where we go.
It's on faces, roofs, meadows, brooks and hooks,
But uplifts the spirit as we recall
that snow is life, the snow is what we like.

Gleams on faces, signs of winter.
Children snowboard, skate and laugh
and make snowmen to the touch.
All they say is, 'Thank you to Thee as today
Thy spirit has come with me.'
Renamed snowday, as this is a spinning day.

Alexia Backhouse (10)
St Christina's School, St John's Wood

SNOW POEM

Snowflakes begin dancing down,
swirling and spinning like angels of winter.
The earth glistens brilliantly,
diamonds are scattered on the ground.
Trees are wrapped up in silvery garments,
protected against the deadly cold.
Blustering, flustering, icy wind,
weaves through forests of trees.
Snow takes over the world.
Each home sparkles, twinkling like crystals.
The last signs of day fade away,
darkness appears instead.
Snowflakes flurry down heavily.
A pearl blanket still remains tranquil, undisturbed.
Picturesque surroundings seem half frozen in time,
delightfully we turn to bed, yearning for day to return.

Roxanna Rezvany (10)
St Christina's School, St John's Wood